FAQs
Regarding New York
DIVORCE
CASES

David I. Bliven, Esq.

Jacobs & Whitehall
9600 Escarpment Blvd
Suite 745-282
Austin, TX 78749
www.jacobsandwhitehall.com

Ordering Information:

Quantity sales. Special discounts are available on quantity purchases by corporations, associations, and others. For details, contact the publisher at the address above.

Orders by U.S. trade bookstores and wholesalers. Please contact Jacobs & Whitehall: Tel: (888) 570-7338 or visit www.jacobsandwhitehall.com.

Printed in the United States of America

Published in 2025

ISBN: 978-1-963063-22-6

PREFACE

Many people have read books like "What to Expect When Expecting." This book - along with my others - are the family law equivalent of that book.

My other books include "Navigating Your New York Divorce Case," Navigating Your New York Family Court Case," "Navigating Your New York High Net Worth Divorce Case," "Navigating Your New York Post-Divorce Case," and "Navigating Your New York Contested Divorce Case." As of the publication of this book, I have a forthcoming book entitled "Navigating Your New York Uncontested Divorce Case."

These books collectively arm a litigant or potential litigant with many of the facts & basic law s/he will need to march down the road of a New York Divorce case or Family Court case.

As I've cautioned in my other volumes, these books do not take the place of a full consultation with a good Family Law attorney – simply because the books provide general information, not case-specific advice. And more importantly these books should not delude you into thinking you can represent yourself – "one who represents oneself has a fool for a client."

Instead, one should see these books for what they are intended to be – helpful supplements. One wouldn't do too well by popping multi-vitamins without eating actual food. Likewise, one should not read these books but then neglect to hire a good family law attorney to represent oneself. If you have children worth having a relationship with and/or assets worth protecting, it's worth having a good attorney at your side.

One other note of caution: this book relates a lot of general precepts and presumptions. With every general rule, there may be a host of exceptions. Thus, one should avoid cherry-picking certain passages out of this book – or any of my books - and treat the passage as gospel.

Finally, this book differs from my other books (as of 2025, "Navigating Your NY Divorce Case," "Navigating Your NY Family Court Case," "Navigating Your NY Contested Divorce Case," "Navigating Your NY Post Divorce Case" and "Navigating Your NY Divorce Agreement Case") in that this book isn't intended to be read primarily from beginning to end. Instead, if one is dealing with a particular issue in one's case, it may make more sense to skip to the particular chapter deadline with that specific issue.

All the best!

Disclaimer

This publication is intended to be used for educational purposes only. No legal advice is being given, and no attorney-client relationship is intended to be created by reading this material. The author assumes no liability for any errors or omissions or for how this book or its contents are used or interpreted, or for any consequences resulting directly or indirectly from the use of this book. For legal or any other advice, please consult an experienced attorney or the appropriate expert, who is aware of the specific facts of your case and is knowledgeable in the law in your jurisdiction.

The Law Offices of David Bliven

www.blivenlaw.net

White Plains Office
140 Grand St.
Suite 402
White Plains, NY 10601
(914) 468-0968

Bronx Office
3190 Riverdale Avenue
Suite 1
Bronx, NY 10463
(718) 725-9600

TABLE OF CONTENTS

CHAPTER 1

TOP 4 MISTAKES TO AVOID WHEN YOU'RE GOING THROUGH A DIVORCE

Mistake Number One: Lack Of Organization

The biggest mistake you can make during a divorce process involves a lack of organization and not having all your documentation ready. The best thing you can do for yourself is to get your paperwork organized beforehand, and go over it with your lawyer.

The paperwork your lawyer will need will include your latest W-2 and most recent tax returns. This will help your lawyer calculate potential child support & maintenance awards - and will allow greater transparency with the other party in the divorce.

Other documents to have on hand include:

- Your latest mortgage statement
- All bank account statements
- Investment account statements
- Retirement account statements

Make sure all these statements are from the most recent month (or if your case has already been filed, from the month the case was filed). Having this up-to-date documentation will allow your lawyer to better determine asset distribution and equity value. It's also important to give your lawyer a timeline of when you and the other party last lived together, and how these living arrangements overlap with financial statements.

Why is this important? It's not uncommon for a client to have last lived with their partner over a year ago, and to have assets that accrued after one party moved out. In that case, your lawyer can look over the dates of marriage, separation, and divorce to argue for helping you keep assets that accrued after separation. Giving your lawyer the full picture and being organized both go a long way in helping you navigate divorce with less stress - and more peace of mind.

Finally, if there were prior orders issued form Family Court, make sure to bring in a copy of those orders when meeting with the attorney. Likewise, if there were prior agreements made (e.g., prenups, post-nups, separation agreements or parenting agreements), bring in copies of those as well.

Mistake Two: Not Meeting Often Enough With Your Lawyer

The next biggest mistake you can make if you're going through a divorce is to avoid meeting with your lawyer. While these meetings can and do take up time, it is much better for both the lawyer and you to be prepared and on the same page.

How often should you meet with your attorney? We recommend scheduling a meeting with your lawyer before each court date. This is especially important if the divorce process involves disputes over things like assets, property, child support, or custody. The more prepared both you and the lawyer are before every court date, the easier it will be for them to understand your perspective and argue your case. You should *also* consider meeting with your lawyer for a "debrief" following each court appearance.

Mistake Three: Assuming Assets In Your Name Can't Be Divided

Many clients assume if a house or an investment account is in their name alone, their spouse can't be awarded any of it. However, this is untrue. In the State of New York, the principle of "equitable distribution" means a spouse can get 50% of "marital assets," even if those assets weren't in both of your names.

Laws in the State of New York define anything that is acquired or increased in ("active") value over the course of the marriage to be an asset which can be divided in a divorce. It's important for you to understand that just because something is in your name alone, it doesn't mean it remains with you in a divorce. Understanding this law can help you be ready for the court process and better equipped to move forward financially.

Mistake Number Four: Not Documenting Spousal Behavior

When your divorce case involves custody or visitation rights, it's very important to document negative behavior from your spouse. This helps your lawyer (and the court) understand your perspective as a parent. But what does this look like, practically speaking?

We recommend when you begin to notice negative changes in your spouse's behavior, you keep a daily journal. This should include written and dated descriptions of events. You should also make records of when you step up to the plate to take your children to doctor's appointments, help them with homework, or take them on play dates *while your spouse does not*. All of this documentation can go a long way in the courtroom and can help your trial move more smoothly.

When dealing with alcohol or substance abuse issues or mental health problems, consistent documentation is especially important. This documentation can take the form of photos, audios or videos of a spouse under the influence, text messages describing the problem and urging your spouse to get help, an audio recording of your spouse making verbal threats or screaming, or paperwork relating to arrests for drug, alcohol, or behavioral offenses.

The more evidence you have, the better we can prepare your case.

CHAPTER 2

3 WARNING SIGNS: BUDGETING FOR UNEXPECTED EXPENSES AFTER DIVORCE

Navigating the financial landscape after a divorce can be especially challenging, particularly when unexpected expenses arise. Being prepared for these unforeseen costs is essential to maintaining financial stability during this transitional period.

In this chapter, I'll highlight three blinking-red warning signs to watch for when budgeting for expenses after a divorce. Recognizing these indicators early on can enable you to take proactive steps to manage your finances effectively, avoid potential pitfalls, and secure a more stable future as you adjust to your new circumstances.

1. **Underestimating Legal and Litigation Costs**

A good number of people I work with are simply unaware of how expensive contested divorce cases in New York are, particularly in higher-cost areas like New York City. Good divorce attorneys in this area can be very expensive, often charging thousands of dollars *per month* - easily $3,000 to $5,000 (& perhaps significantly more in high income or high net worth cases[1]).

---

[1] Indeed, in high income cases, I've seen counsel fees average $10-20,000 monthly. In ultra-high net worth cases (incomes exceeding $1 million and assets in the tens of millions), attorneys fees can exceed $100,000 per month.

Although it's rare for divorce cases to go to trial[2], you'd do well to budget $30,000 to $50,000. Add to your divorce contested custody and contested financial issues, and you're easily looking at twice that amount or more (even if your case is not a high-income case).

Be prepared for these expenses by setting aside a significant budget for legal fees. Understand that the combined household income will be stretched thin post-separation, and plan accordingly.

2. Adjusting To The Financial Realities Of Single Living

Once you separate, the financial support previously pooled into a single household must now support two separate households, drastically reducing any additional funds you'd otherwise have. Unexpected living expenses, not to mention rent,

[2] Roughly 95-98% of family law cases settle at some point.

utilities, and transportation, can add up quickly and strain your budget.

You might need to consider moving to a more affordable location or even living with a roommate or relative temporarily to manage costs. For example, a family in Westchester might need to relocate to a less expensive area like Yonkers, despite the impact on lifestyle and convenience.

Conduct a thorough budget analysis with a financial planner, considering net income, potential maintenance, and child support obligations (or receipt of same). This will help you understand what areas and housing options are financially feasible.

3. Failing To Utilize Professional Financial Planning

Divorce often involves complex financial arrangements that require specialized knowledge beyond what a typical divorce attorney can provide. Decisions related to your divorce, such as asset division, maintenance, and child support, will significantly impact your financial future.

Determining whether to prioritize maintenance over child support, or how to divide assets optimally, can be challenging without professional advice. A Certified Divorce Financial Planner (CDFA)[3] can provide you with tailored advice, ensuring that settlements are structured in your best financial interest.

It's wise to hire a CDFA as early in the process as possible to assist with the complex financial planning you'll have to do. They can help you negotiate the most beneficial mix of assets and support, considering long-term financial stability rather than just a straightforward 50/50 asset split.

Some Additional Tips:

- **Regular Financial Check-ins:** Schedule regular check-ins with your financial planner and/or

---

[3] https://institutedfa.com/

your attorney to reassess your budget and adjust for any changes in income or expenses.

- **Emergency Fund:** Establish an emergency fund as soon as possible to cover unexpected expenses unrelated to the divorce that might arise during or after the divorce process.

CHAPTER 3

TOP 3 FINANCIAL MISTAKES DURING A DIVORCE

What Are The Most Common Financial Mistakes To Avoid During Divorce?

Mistake #1: Many people assume if they simply shift money into a sole account from a joint account, they won't have to share or split that money. This is untrue. In the State of New York, your assets are presumptively divided equally (especially in a marriage lasting more than a few years), regardless of whose name is on an account or title. The same is true of investments and retirement savings.

If you're counting your paycheck as "solely your income" - think again. Once you say "I do" then your money is his money and his money is your money. In the case of alimony payments and child support, you should also look at investment income and income from rental properties, if applicable. Once that added income is put into a sole account and you file taxes separately from a spouse, this now counts as income your spouse may be entitled to, even if the rental property is jointly shared.

Mistake #2: Another common financial mistake is to keep earning as much as you can, working overtime, and raking in bonuses at work, even when you sense a divorce is on the horizon. While you may be doing this in hopes of having enough saved up to get by after the marriage is over, what you're really doing is earning more for the other party to take a share of.

The same can often be said for bonuses earned after a divorce case is filed. While some performance-based bonuses may be exempt, your bonuses are often considered marital property - along with a percentage accrued to your income. Thus, 50% of your bonus for that given year (even those earned after filing for a divorce) can still be awarded to a spouse during proceedings.

Mistake #3: The same holds true for 401k accounts. If you're contributing to a 401k account even after a divorce is filed, you're piling up money that a spouse can later claim half of. It's wisest to set up a frozen "marital" account to keep these assets separate and segregate out post-filing contributions to your 401k.

Dividing out passive appreciation or the interest from a 401k can get complicated. Similarly, distinguishing interest from a separate property or post commencement portion of your 401k can be difficult. Often, the distinction isn't made, and your spouse could walk away with more than they really should.

What Can You Do To Protect Yourself In This Situation?

Meet with an accountant or a financial planner with a background in the financial aspects of divorce cases. Get the right kind of advice so you get the best input on how to handle your assets carefully and wisely, both before and after a divorce case is filed.

CHAPTER 4

TOP 5 WAYS TO PROTECT YOUR FINANCIAL INTEREST BEFORE, DURING, AND AFTER A NEW YORK DIVORCE

What Are The Best Strategies To Protect My Assets During A Divorce?

Contact a divorce attorney as early as possible in the process - ideally before filing. It's also wise to consult an accountant, a personal financial planner, and a wealth protection advisor. If you have children, consider setting up a 529 plan to help pay for their college education and protect those funds from division.

New York law mandates that assets be distributed fairly and equitably in a divorce, but "fair" can often feel subjective to those going through the process.

To safeguard funds in your business account from being distributed, consider reinvesting them back into your business, particularly if you own a small business. Be mindful of the amounts you pay yourself in the months or years leading up to a divorce, and consider directing those funds into marketing and advertising.

Why is this important? Any money deposited into bank accounts, investment accounts, or retirement accounts while married is generally subject to a 50-50 division with your spouse. Work closely with a wealth protection advisor and a certified divorce financial planner to strategically allocate your money and minimize the impact on your assets.

What Distinguishes Marital Property From Separate Property?

Marital property is simply any property that is either acquired or accrues active value during the time in a marriage. Separate property is any property or assets that you owned prior to the marriage. It can also include some property accrued after the marriage, such as gifts that are clearly made to one spouse or an inheritance.

So long as that property is not commingled with marital assets, it may be considered separate property. However, marital property is the general presumption in New York, and an attorney can review your assets and help you better understand the distinctions pertaining to your case.

How Do I Protect Separate Property From Being Divided In A Divorce?

Make sure your separate property is segregated. If you receive an inheritance or a settlement payment, it's wisest to deposit that money into a fully separate, brand new savings account in your name alone. Then leave it alone! Adding money from joint accounts will commingle the account, making it fair game in a divorce.

1. What Role Do Trusts And Other Legal Tools Play In Protecting Assets During A Divorce?

Trusts may not protect assets as well as you think they will. For example, if a trust is in your name alone but some amount of money in the trust comes from marital assets, the entire trust amount is now distributable.

A trust that is entirely separate from marital assets and takes in nothing from shared income streams can be described as truly separate property, however[4]. You may also wish to structure your trust to pay you out after a certain period of time has gone by to avoid this amount being claimed during divorce.

---

[4] If one inherits retirement assets from a (now deceased) relative, one may set-up an "Inherited IRA" account to help preserve its separate property character. Just be sure not to deposited any of your own funds into that account.

This can be especially helpful if you have assets from a personal injury settlement or similar awards.

What Steps Can I Take To Manage My Finances During And After A Divorce?

Make sure you hire a good divorce attorney as early in the process as possible, along with a forensic accountant. Get in touch with a certified divorce financial planner and a wealth protection advisor to help you manage your finances and plan ahead in light of a divorce.

Your financial planner can examine your current income and expenditure and factor in future post-divorce expenses to suggest a truly equitable and fairer division plan. This can help you come out in better financial shape in the long run.

Your financial planner can also help you budget for future child support and spousal maintenance payments and work to find you a financially prudent, agreeable new neighborhood to live in. This helps protect you through a divorce and beyond and move ahead with far fewer financial concerns.

CHAPTER 5

STRATEGIC FINANCIAL MOVES IN YOUR DIVORCE

Your Key To Financial Clarity

Initiating a divorce and navigating the immediate repercussions means you're bombarded with countless decisions. When weighing up how to tackle these financial matters prior to your New York divorce fully wrapping up, you may wonder whether you should open up new bank accounts and lines of credit.

It can be sensible to open new accounts, such as credit cards in your name, before filing for divorce. Keep in mind, however, it isn't *necessary* that you do. The rationale here would be to establish clear distinctions between *pre-commencement* and *post-commencement* assets and debts once the divorce proceedings begin.

Allow me to illustrate a little more plainly. Let's say you had a checking account or a credit card account during your marriage – even if only your name was on the account & not your spouse's. When you file for divorce, you want all the associated debt and assets to be considered as post-commencement. However, there could be complications. For instance, if you continue to use a joint account or credit card during the divorce process, opposing counsel might argue the funds or debts incurred post-commencement are still marital assets.

A recent case I had comes to mind. In it, my client deposited their income into a bank account while still married. After they filed for divorce, which ended up dragging out for years, they used funds from this account to make a down payment on a second house. Despite the clear separation in timing between the divorce filing and the house purchase, opposing counsel argued the funds were commingled, making it challenging (from their perspective) to discern whether they were marital or separate assets.

While I firmly believe this argument is flawed because of the clarity of the New York statute on the matter - that is, the provisions that freeze assets at the time of divorce filing - it's wise to avoid these issues altogether. Depositing your income into a separate account ensures commingling doesn't happen whatsoever and that the funds become clearly recognizable as post-commencement. On top of this, separate accounts can shield your finances from potential misuse or debt accumulation by the other party, which isn't entirely uncommon.

Accepting Money From Others

Accepting money from family or friends during your divorce process should not automatically be considered joint funds that your spouse can claim. Generally, any money or assets acquired after the filing of the divorce case are considered separate funds.

However, to avoid any potential complications or arguments from the opposing side, (especially if the amount is significant), I recommend setting up a completely separate account for the received funds. Whether it's an inheritance, a gift, or any other form of financial assistance, segregating the money in a separate account ensures clarity and avoids confusion surrounding categorizing the funds as commingled.

Another consideration is how accepting funds from family or friends might impact your divorce case, particularly if it affects your employment status. For instance, if you quit your job or accept a lower-paying job and rely on financial support from relatives, your spouse may argue that this support should be considered as part of your income for purposes such as child support.

I've represented a father who either quit his job or was fired and was supported by his parents afterward. This had many implications for the child support case that followed. The mother argued the financial support provided by his parents should be considered as his income, and quite frankly, it's the same exact argument I would have made if I were representing her.

Before you accept any substantial financial assistance, it's important you consult with an attorney. They can provide guidance on the potential impact on your case and advise on the best course of action to protect your interests.

CHAPTER 6

BREAKING FREE FINANCIALLY

When You Have a Spouse with Complete Financial Control

Navigating the complexities of divorce, especially when your spouse holds financial control, can feel like an uphill battle. Seeking legal counsel can help, but it doesn't magically change the fact that you're still financially dependent, *at best*. Fortunately, there are courses you can pursue, even if you find yourself in these circumstances. If you need to hire a divorce attorney without your spouse knowing, consider the following avenues of recourse before giving up as you trudge through the many financial considerations in your New York divorce.

- **Apply For A Credit Card**

  If your spouse is the primary earner or controls most of the assets, you can apply for a credit card using their income and assets on the application. Since marital property is presumed to be jointly owned, even if it's titled solely in your spouse's name, you can include this information on the credit card application without fear of doing so being considered credit card fraud.

- **Borrow From Family or Friends**

  If you're unable to secure a credit card, you can borrow money from family members or friends to fund your legal representation. This can provide you with the necessary resources to hire an attorney without needing to involve your spouse.

- **Legal Financing Companies**

  If you can't get what you need from family and friends for whatever reason, consider looking into a company that specializes in providing loans for legal expenses. They will assess your case and may offer you a loan based on the potential outcome of your divorce proceedings. However, be cautious of the terms and conditions associated with these loans.

In one experience, I was able to assist a client who was only around 18 years old at the time, with no significant assets or employment history to his name. Despite this, a legal financing company evaluated the potential case and gave him a $20,000 loan based on the estimated outcome of approximately $100,000.

As enticing as this may sound, it's essential you approach such arrangements with caution. Legal financing companies typically secure their loans with a lien on the potential proceeds of the case, and borrowers are required to sign loan agreements detailing terms and conditions, including provisions for repayment and consequences for default.

- **Office Of The Self-Represented**

Many Supreme Courts (particularly in the greater New York City area) have offices dedicated to assisting individuals who cannot afford legal representation. You can seek help from volunteer attorneys who may assist you in drafting motions for counsel fees or assign you a pro bono attorney. The Office of the Self-Represented is where you can find this assistance.

This application, known as a "poor person motion," typically requires an affidavit stating the applicant's lack of income, property, or assets available for legal expenses. It should also outline previous attempts made to secure funding, including unsuccessful attempts to secure a loan. The purpose of this motion is to request the assignment of a pro bono attorney and assistance with legal fees.

Once an attorney is assigned, they will review the details of your case, including income, assets, and properties involved. If it becomes evident your spouse is the party with greater financial resources, the attorney may proceed to file a counsel fee application to ensure fair representation and compensation for their services in the case. This process aims to ensure access to legal representation for all facing financial constraints during legal proceedings.

If both spouses face financial challenges, securing funds to hire a private attorney might prove difficult, if not impossible. If you find yourself in this situation, you may need to consider representing yourself or seeking assistance from pro bono attorneys or legal aid organizations. While the Legal Aid Society does provide representation for individuals with limited financial means in divorce cases, their resources may be relatively limited.

Explore these options and determine the best course of action for your specific circumstances before losing hope. Hiring an experienced divorce attorney is important for protecting your interests during the divorce process, and these avenues can help you access legal representation even if your spouse controls the finances.

Loans

Taking out loans before or during a divorce to cover living expenses and attorney fees is, from a legal perspective, a low-risk thing you can do if you need to. Here are some possibilities to consider when weighing up the pros and cons of doing so:

- **Bank Loans**

Banks may extend loans based on your assets or property, even if they are considered marital property, as mentioned earlier. Discuss the particulars with your bank (and/or financial planner) to explore options before taking any loan, though.

- **Home Equity Loans**

If you have property in your name, you can request a home equity loan. However, if the property is jointly owned, you may need your spouse's permission or court approval.

Before taking out any loans, it's essential to consult with your attorney. They can provide guidance on the best course of action (from the legal perspective) and help explore alternatives.

Finally, you may be eligible to request counsel fees, alimony, or child support from the court, which could alleviate the need for a loan. Some attorneys will agree to take your case on a reduced fee - and thus promptly make an application to the Judge requiring your spouse to reimbursement the attorney’s fees s/he would otherwise charge to you. Discussing your options with an attorney can help you make informed decisions regarding your financial situation during the divorce process.

CHAPTER 7

WAYS TO PROTECT YOUR BUSINESS BEFORE, DURING, & AFTER A NEW YORK DIVORCE

As A New York Business Owner, What Legal Aspects Should I Consider During A Divorce?

The first thing to consider during a divorce is the size of your business. How big is your business, and what kind of structure does it have? It's a good idea to let your business partners or co-officers know about the divorce beforehand so they understand the situation and are not surprised by visits from your spouse or their attorney.

If you are an equity partner or have a sizable percentage ownership of a corporation, the next question to ask is whether your business was started during the marriage. If so, your spouse may have a share in the business and be entitled to a percentage as part of the divorce.

You may also wish to meet with an experienced wealth protection advisor to determine how to best protect your company and its assets through a divorce. Be sure to get in touch with a certified divorce financial planner and an accountant, as well, to make sure your company's finances are in order and to plan for the divorce.

Can My Business Be Considered A Marital Asset?

Generally speaking, a business started during the marriage is considered marital property and a divisible asset.

If your business was started before marriage but has grown considerably during the time you were married, this is known as "appreciation of active value" - a percentage of this value may be considered a marital asset, as well.

For example, suppose your business was only worth $100,000 at the time of marriage but has grown to a million-dollar business throughout the marriage. In that case, your spouse may be entitled to a percentage of the "active appreciation."

A forensic accountant would be needed to determine the value. If the issues cannot be settled by a forensic accountant, a Judge will weigh in and give their determination as to the overall active appreciation of your business.

Will New York's Equitable Distribution Law Affect My Business Assets?

New York Law requires assets to be split equitably or fairly between a divorcing couple. Even if your spouse had nothing to do with the foundation and growth of your business over the years, they may still be entitled to up to 50% or more of the value of your business.

It's important to get in touch with a divorce attorney, wealth protection advisor, accountant, and financial planner as early in the process as possible. If possible, while divorce is still looming and has not yet been filed for. This early preparation will put you in a better position to protect your business assets and prepare your business for the financial aspect of the divorce.

How Will My Business Be Valued During A Divorce?

A business is valued by a forensic accountant, who will have a list of documents they will ask your business to produce. They will ask for, among other things, tax returns, schedules, bank account records, asset listings and financial statements from audits or appraisals.

They will also ask for information on ledgers and employee payments. If anyone owes your business money or if your business owes anyone money, documents related to those debts will be requested.

The forensic accountant will also ask for a list of fixed assets, such as real estate investments, and may request appraisals. Documentation related to distribution to shareholders will also be sought, and information related to marketing and advertising may be requested, as well.

All of this data will be used to value your business and evaluate its growth history and finances during the time you were married.

How Might Divorce Impact Me Financially As A Business Owner?

On a personal level, if you have children, you may be asked to pay child support or spousal maintenance if there is a significant difference between your respective earnings. Some business owners don't see a divorce coming and mix personal and business expenses, e.g., using a business account to make personal vehicle payments.

This can be disastrous and land you in serious trouble with the other party's forensic accountant, costing you considerably during a divorce. Make sure your business and personal expenses are clearly separated and have all documentation for valid business expenses (such as receipts, invoices, and bills) ready.

How Can Divorce Impact My Business' Cash Flow And Operations?

The enormous effort it will take you to comb through years of documents can be a huge distraction which may negatively impact cash flow. For that reason, one should consider hiring a forensic accountant of one's own (aside from the court-assigned neutral). Your accountant can communicate with your spouse's accountant and help streamline the document-seeking process, leaving you freer to focus on running your business.

The less distracted you and your team are, the less "normal business proceedings" will be impacted. Hiring a forensic accountant to communicate with one's attorney and with the other party's accountant will take a considerable burden off of your shoulders and allow cash flow to continue more normally.

What Other Steps Can I Take To Protect My Business Before And During A Divorce?

Be prepared for the divorce as early as possible. If you own a larger business worth millions, tens of millions, or hundreds of millions, begin to assemble a team early. Get an attorney, an accountant (for tax advice purposes), a certified divorce financial planner, a wealth protection advisor, and a forensic accountant.

Your divorce attorney can also help you better understand the documents and professional help you will need to assemble your case. Your attorney can also coordinate with your forensic accountant to streamline the process and get the documentation you'll need ahead of the divorce.

This lets you, as a business owner, focus on your business with fewer distractions and allows you a much less stressful divorce when that bridge is crossed.

CHAPTER 8

SOCIAL MEDIA ETIQUETTE DURING DIVORCE: DOS AND DON'TS

What Are Some Things To Do Or Not Do On Social Media During Or Pre-Divorce?

Navigating social media can be a minefield when you're going through a divorce or even before the process officially begins, so it's vital to be cautious about what you share online. In fact, one of the biggest mistakes you can make during a divorce case is to speak negatively about your spouse or children online.

This can backfire spectacularly, especially if your spouse has the means to hire an IT expert. They can dig up not only your current posts but also anything you've deleted. So, if you've ever posted something you regret, like a photo that puts you in a bad light, it's wise to delete it and consider getting professional help to clean up your digital footprint.

What's more, concerns about your digital presence are not limited to what you say about your family. You should steer entirely clear of discussing your divorce case on social media. Anything you post can be used against you in court, and Judges are not impressed by litigants airing their grievances online. It could even lead to a court order restricting your social media use, which is the last thing you need when you're already dealing with the stress of a divorce.

Then there's the issue of your personal life. Posting about late-night parties or other behavior could be seen as irresponsible, especially when you're supposed to be caring for your children – and thus is a big no-no. Your posts can contradict your statements in court and damage your credibility.

The best approach is to discuss your social media use with your attorney. They can give you specific advice on what to post and what to avoid, ensuring your online activity doesn't harm your case. Remember, a little caution on social media can go a long way in protecting your interests during a divorce.

CHAPTER 9

TOP 5 STEPS YOU CAN TAKE TO SAFEGUARDING YOUR DIGITAL LIFE FOR A DIVORCE

Navigating the precarious journey of divorce requires safeguarding your personal, financial documents and digital life.

Here's a list of the top things you can do:

1. Start with a sweep through your social media privacy settings—it's more crucial than you think. But don't stop there; change your

passwords on absolutely everything. We're talking emails, text messages, iCloud, social media—leave no stone unturned. And if you're still under the same roof as your soon-to-be ex, consider maintaining a digital distance. Use a separate computer if possible, and definitely update those passwords on all your gadgets, be it laptops, iPads, or even the family desktop.

2. Another piece of advice that often slips under the radar? Ditch the face recognition feature on your devices. Why, you ask? Imagine your spouse, under the cover of night, using your sleeping face to unlock your secrets. It's not just a scene from a spy movie; it's a real threat, especially in those high-stakes divorces. And for those navigating particularly contentious or affluent separations, bringing in an IT expert might just be your best defense. They can clean up your digital footprint, ensuring your posts, photos, and videos are locked down tight, away from prying eyes.

3. Now, if you're sharing tech with your spouse, know this: it's not illegal to snoop through shared devices for documents. So, protect your findings. Copy them, stash them in a secure folder, and slap a password on it. Personal security doesn't stop at two-factor authentication, either. One can go a step further with three-factor authentication for one's most sensitive files[5]. Even if someone manages to hack into my devices, they're hitting a digital wall.
4. Secure your financial paperwork. Scan everything and store it in the cloud, protected behind a password with two-factor authentication—this is non-negotiable. And don't forget about your spouse's documents; if they're lying around, they're fair game. Screen capture and scan those too.

---

[5] For example, setting up 2-factor authentication to get into the device itself, then within the device, protect individual files/folders with a password.

5. Worried about securing specific files or documents? It's simpler than you think. A quick Google search can teach you how to password-protect an Adobe document in about ten seconds flat. Remember, in the digital arena of divorce, your offense is a good defense.

CHAPTER 10

PROTECTING PARENTAL RIGHTS WHEN DIVORCE IS ON THE HORIZON

What Are The Best Ways To Protect Your Parental Rights?

Parental rights tend to cover the issues of custody and of visitation rights. Taking the right steps before a divorce is crucial to retaining access to your kids, and making a strong case in court.

One of the first steps you should take is to make sure, if or when you initially move out, you take the children with you. If you don't, you've already given your spouse a leg up in physical custody proceedings, as they can simply say "Well, he or she has already abandoned the children, so it seems they're better off with me, anyway."

Another key way to protect parental rights if you're expecting a custody debate is to simply spend as much time with your children as possible. Don't carry on as normal; spend one-on-one time with your kids, take them to ball games, drive them to school & appointments. Go the extra mile.

Otherwise, your spouse's attorney could simply point out that their client has spent 60-70% of the time with the kids, whereas you've spent only 40% at best. They'll pull out calendars with dates and times, and that will be counted as evidence in court.

If you're looking at joint custody as the likely outcome, you should make sure you're very involved in every aspect of your children's lives long before the divorce process is underway.

What does this involved parenting look like? This means…

- Going to extracurricular activities
- Setting up playdates
- Taking the kids to doctor's visits
- Participating as much as the other parent

Without active participation, it becomes easy for the other party to simply reply in court that you're not actually all that involved and don't deserve joint custody. Active, meaningful participation will allow witnesses (such as a doctor, coach, or teacher) to testify that you're an attentive and caring parent. Remember, a Judge will see little point in joint custody if one parent seems to be absent and uninvolved. Showing up and helping out goes a long way.

How can you better your case in terms of visitation rights? Apart from simply being attentive and involved as a parent, if you have personal struggles, be sure to address these as early as possible. See a therapist if you have mental health issues. This allows the court to see that even if you struggle, you're actively getting help and being responsible. A letter from a therapist highlighting your progress and commitment to wellness can have a positive impact, too.

Some parents struggle more than others. If you expect the other party may allege you have a drug or alcohol problem, check into a rehab center. Let the center know you have a divorce on the horizon, and get an assessment from them as to whether or not you need treatment.

If their screening confirms you don't need treatment, get a letter from the center stating as much; this will be a great help in court. If they determine you do, in fact, need treatment, get that help immediately. The sooner you address and actively work on your issues, the better off you'll be in visitation hearings.

Finally, make sure you have a caring, competent, and thorough attorney on your side. Getting the right voice in court is crucial to making sure your parental concerns and rights are heard, protected and professionally represented.

CHAPTER 11

TOP 3 MISTAKES TO AVOID IN A CUSTODY DISPUTE

Mistake One: Waiting Too Long To Hire An Attorney

The biggest mistake you can make in a divorce case involving children is to wait to hire an attorney. Many clients feel they can handle custody arrangements on their own, and don't plan to hire an attorney unless their spouse contests terms after the process is underway.

Unfortunately, trying to petition for custody or understand how to effectively petition without a lawyer present from the beginning can be ruinous. A good lawyer can understand what information, facts, and evidence need to be submitted, while a spouse may feel unsure whether or not they should include certain details.

It is common for a custody journey that feels friendly at first to becomes difficult, unpleasant, and competitive once you get to court. A spouse with a good custody lawyer has a professional with the legal backing, familiarity with the law, and understanding of documentation needed to fight well. On the other hand, a spouse with no lawyer only has their word (and little more) to defend them and their children.

Don't let that be you. Remember, it's always safest to enter this journey prepared, and well-represented, from the beginning. The sooner you hire a family law attorney, the sooner we can go over your case, and help you compile the right information.

Mistake Two: Hiding Or Omitting Information

When facing divorce, you may feel tempted to withhold upsetting details about your spouse's behavior in an attempt to keep things amicable or avoid angering them. But all details about a spouse's negative behavior, addictions, mental health issues, and legal history should always be disclosed from the beginning.

The more accurate and detailed information your attorney can compile from the start, the safer your children will be in the long-run. Remember, the goal is not to pity or protect an abusive or problematic spouse, but to fight for your rights as a parent and keep your children safe.

The easiest way for your attorney to do that is with honest, consistent records of mental health, addiction, behavioral, and legal issues. This documentation could take the form of:

- Text messages from a spouse admitting to dangerous or illegal behavior

- Photos or videos documenting a drinking problem, drug use, violence, or neglect
- Audio recordings of aggressive or threatening language
- Formal paperwork linked to arrests
- Dated journal entries documenting your spouse's concerning behavior
- And more…

Submitting this information with the original petition keeps your case consistent, and allows your attorney to enter the custody dispute far better prepared. Omitting references in your initial application to things like "Father has a drug addiction" will likely come back to bite you[6]. Finally, you and your attorney can sit down and focus on the financial aspects of your custody dispute, making sure to help you avoid the third most common mistake clients often make.

---

[6] As a practical matter, if you omit such items, any Judge will question why you did so – which then undercuts the credibility of those accusations.

Mistake Three: Underestimating Legal Costs

Custody litigation can be lengthy and costly. A responsible lawyer will sit down with clients to discuss finances, before they even get to court. While a good attorney can help you prepare to win, you also need to be prepared to handle the expenses of a custody dispute.

What might those expenses look like? Upfront retainer fees can range from $10,000 to $25,000 (or more) for good family law attorneys – but this doesn't include later billed hours. Keep in mind that a lawyer can easily bill 100 hours or more once your case goes to court, and if your attorney costs $600 to $1,200 an hour, costs will add up over time. Documents, records, subpoenas, and witnesses may need to be secured, and this will increase expenses, too.

Having a realistic and strong plan in place to pay for fees is important; being unable to continue paying for a lawyer mid-trial can damage an otherwise strong case. We don't tell you this to scare you, only to help you decide how to best use your resources (such as lines of credit, savings, or assets), and to understand that being prepared will increase your chances of success.

So, what's next? The healthiest thing you can do for your case is to sit down today with a knowledgeable and seasoned family law attorney. We can discuss the details of your case, the strength of your custody dispute, and any other questions you may have. Coming equipped with proper documentation, financial plans, and evidence of a spouse's problematic behavior will go a long way in helping you and your lawyer argue your custody case together.

CHAPTER 12

TOP 8 TIPS FOR PREPARING FOR A CHILD CUSTODY HEARING

How Can I Gather And Organize Important Documents For My Case?

One of the first things you should do is to begin to document communication between parties and streamline your plans for childcare and child support payments.

Two apps that I recommend for this purpose are "Our Family Wizard[7]" and "2 Houses[8]." These apps automatically organize information, making it much easier for a Judge or lawyer to understand and follow.

Keeping a journal can also be helpful in documenting day-to-day activities and documenting how you parent[9]. This is especially helpful if you are the primary parent who assumes most or all of the parenting and caregiving roles your child needs.

Be sure to document in your journal when you wake up, when your child wakes up, when they eat, and who feeds and dresses the child. Keep track of all daily responsibilities from morning through evening -

---

[7] https://www.ourfamilywizard.com/

[8] https://www.2houses.com/en/

[9] There are numerous such journals available on Amazon: https://www.amazon.com/s?k=child+custody+journal&i=stripbooks&crid=3IIPY9TWXS2Y0&sprefix=child+custody+journal%2Cstripbooks%2C48&ref=nb_sb_noss_1.

note how many of these tasks you do and how many the other party does.

Be sure to get third-party corroboration from doctors, teachers, and coaches verifying that you are the one bringing your child to appointments, school, or sporting practice. This usually takes the form of letters and affidavits affirming that you are caring for your child and showing up, visibly making sure your child's needs are met.

How Do I Prepare For Questions About My Parenting Abilities?

Sit down with your attorney and go through mock scenarios. Your attorney will ask you what negative things the other party may say about you and help prepare you for cross-examination in light of negative or critical feedback.

Have testimony & evidence ready to rebut accusations from the other party. For example, if the other party is going to accuse you of being mentally unstable, be sure to have letters from a therapist or counselor ready to help a Judge understand what you struggle with and what your limits vs. strengths are.

These letters can also help a Judge understand that your anxiety, for example, was linked primarily to the bad marriage and after moving out, your mental health is significantly improved and won't impact your parenting.

How Can I Best Present Myself In Court?

Wear what you would for an important job interview; at the very least, dress business casual. For a male, that will mean a collared button-down shirt, slacks, and dress shoes. For a female, a blouse with a pantsuit or business-appropriate blouse and skirt.

You may find yourself getting hot sitting in a full suit all day in court, so a full suit isn't necessarily advised. But be sure to be neat, tidily dressed, with excellent hygiene & hair combed - this lets the Judge know you are taking this seriously and want to create the best possible impression.

What Role Does Documentation Of Communication With The Other Parent Play?

Documentation is critical. Documentation helps refute the other side's possible accusations of poor parenting. The more of your involvement with your child you document, the better your case will be. To this end, the previously mentioned parenting apps are helpful.

A paper trail with apps, texts, and emails is important. If your spouse has been violent, be sure to reach out to them via text or email about their violence, letting them know why you feel the child would be unsafe with them and writing out specific examples of abuse.

Their silence or non-argument of the case in response can be taken as proof those accusations are true.

What Should I Know About The Role Of Child Custody Evaluators?

Child custody evaluators (a/k/a forensic psychologists) have a very important role to play in determining custody and the outcomes of your case. Be sure to sit down with your attorney to understand what questions the evaluator will ask and what tests they will use to attempt to determine your fitness as a parent.

Be sure to determine what the evaluator has decided or recommended, and consider lining up your own forensic evaluator in light of those issues. Your attorney can walk you through this entire process to help you be ready to answer questions, understand the process ahead of time, and review the outcome of these evaluations[10].

---

[10] For a brief outline of what to expect, checkout this article: https://www.afccnet.org/Resource-Center/Family-Resources/Preparing-for-your-Custody-Evaluation

What Are The Common Mistakes To Avoid During A Custody Hearing?

Don't denigrate or try to tear down the other party. This can be difficult to do, as tensions often run high, but be sure to work on your anger response and avoid pushing the other party's buttons.

Be sure to work on any negative factors that you have against you. This might include mental health issues, drug or alcohol issues, or anger management problems. Get help for these problems, and be sure to carefully document the help you are getting.

A Judge won't necessarily look negatively on merely attending therapy or Alcoholics Anonymous - unless you are inadequately addressing your issues. If anything, getting this help shows you are working at bettering yourself and getting healthy so you can be a better parent and get the treatment you need.

Getting this treatment can also help provide the nuanced opinions and diagnosis of a specialist. For example, your therapist can counter accusations of "He or she is crazy" with a response of "This person is getting help for depression and anxiety, is making notable strides with the help of medication and therapy, and their issues won't impact parenting at all."

How Can I Create A Strong And Realistic Parenting Plan?

Begin with a map of what your child's week looks like. Appointments, school, timings, and activity days. Next, determine how a decision is going to be made and how that will be communicated. Follow this careful process month by month, covering holidays, school weeks, summer vacation, and weekends.

Decide what you will do if the other parent neglects their responsibilities. Will you go to mediation? Or hire a parenting coordinator?

Address possible scenarios such as your child being in the hospital, a parent relocating, overnight periods away from home, and staying with relatives. A good, strong, parenting plan goes on for dozens of pages and covers every possible parenting situation in detail and workably. An attorney can also help you review your parenting plan and make sure that it's strong and comprehensive.

How Can A New York Family Attorney Assist In Preparation Efforts?

A good New York family law attorney is going to have model parenting plan agreements on their computer ready to go. This allows you to sit down with such plans and decide which aspects of it you would like to use. With this outline in hand, you can begin to negotiate with the other party on a middle ground that works for each of you and, above all, for your child.

CHAPTER 13

10 SIGNS YOU NEED TO SEEK EMERGENCY CUSTODY IN NEW YORK

How Does The Court Determine Whether Emergency Custody Is Necessary In New York?

The courts will consider the seriousness of the allegations and how well those allegations are corroborated. In some cases, especially if there are simply threats from your spouse to take the children, all that's needed is for a Judge to establish a firm parental access schedule to protect both of your parental rights.

However, if the other party has significant issues, such as mental health problems, violent tendencies, drug or alcohol use, or anger management issues, these can warrant a temporary emergency custody application. To have that application approved, it's important to have evidence of your claims.

What might that evidence look like? If your spouse has a serious drinking problem, evidence can include photos of empty alcohol bottles, videos of your spouse inebriated, paperwork showing a DWI conviction, or letters from a rehab center.

Without this evidence, it's easy for your spouse to simply come before a Judge and say, "Yes, I drink, but I don't have a problem." You'll need to be able to back up your claims to have a successful application for temporary emergency custody.

What Steps Should I Take If I Suspect My Child Is In Danger When They're With Their Other Parent?

If you have solid evidence your child has been physically or sexually abused, you need to report it to the police or to Child Protective Services. If you suspect your child is being abused but aren't sure or don't have proof, reaching out to a lawyer first can be helpful. Your attorney can discuss your concerns and help you decide what the next best move is, especially in high-conflict situations.

It's important to be aware that solid evidence of abuse is needed to obtain temporary emergency custody. In many cases, the best way to corroborate abuse is to take your child to a doctor. It can be difficult for a lawyer or a Judge to determine if abuse is or is not occurring, and a doctor can determine if the marks on your child's body or their complaints of pain or harm are evidence of abuse.

Can I File For Emergency Custody Without A Family Law Attorney In New York?

Yes, it is possible to file for emergency custody without the help of a lawyer. These forms can be found on the New York Courts website[11], and you can also go to a family court for help drafting and filing the petition.

However, having an attorney's help can play a crucial role in the success of your application. A family lawyer will have a better sense of the strength of your allegations and the strength of evidence against your spouse. An attorney can then help you understand what to include in the form.

It's always best to at least consult with an attorney before you file, as they can best guide you on how to legally and successfully advocate for and protect your child if you suspect or determine that they are in danger.

---

11 https://www.nycourts.gov/LegacyPDFS/FORMS/familycourt/pdfs/gf-1.pdf

What Evidence Do I Need To Support An Emergency Custody Request?

No initial evidence is *needed* to fill out the form, but if you do have physical evidence of abuse or neglect, this can be attached to or submitted with the petition. An order to show cause along with the application can help you request a Temporary Restraining Order on the same day that you petition for emergency custody[12], and an attorney can guide you through that process.

The affidavit accompanying your order must also explain why you did not notify the other parent of the request, and your evidence of abuse or neglect will go a long way in explaining your urgency and demonstrating the seriousness of the situation. Your attorney can also guide you in filling out the fact sheet

---

12
https://www.nycourts.gov/LegacyPDFS/FORMS/familycourt/pdfs/gf-5b.pdf

of your order to show cause and wording your affidavit for the best chances of success.

How Long Does It Take To Get An Emergency Custody Order In New York?

In especially serious cases with ample evidence, the emergency custody order could be granted on the same day. Normally, however, a Judge will ask to hear from the other party before they issue an emergency order. In this case, they'll provide you with a date a few days to a few weeks out to hear both sides of the dispute.

In many cases with ample evidence, a Temporary Restraining Order can be put in effect until your court date to prevent further contact while still allowing a Judge to hear what the other party has to say.

What Should I Expect During An Emergency Custody Hearing?

Emergency custody hearings are handled differently than standard custody trials. In these hearings, Judges may allow forms of evidence that wouldn't typically be permitted at a full trial, such as affidavit evidence or hearsay. The Judge may also restrict the hearing's duration, sometimes allotting just 15 to 30 minutes per side to present their case, given the urgency of the situation and the limited time available.

Because of the potential for a child to be in danger, Judges often accommodate these hearings outside regular hours. You may be called to appear early in the morning or after the day's last hearing to ensure your claim is heard. It's important to make yourself available as needed to demonstrate the seriousness of your case and ensure the Judge has the opportunity to review your concerns.

What Role Does CPS Play In Emergency Custody Cases?

Child Protective Services may or may not play a role, depending on whether they have been contacted in advance. In other cases, a Judge may call for a Court Ordered Investigation by Child Protective Services to investigate the allegations of abuse or neglect.

Child Protective Services may indeed report to the Judge they have found evidence of abuse. Even if they did not find direct evidence of abuse, they may note other issues of concern and include these findings in their report.

What Can I Do If The Emergency Custody Request Is Denied?

The first thing to do is to file an appeal. You can file an emergency appeal and an emergency order with any evidence or new evidence of abuse or neglect. However, it's important to talk with your family lawyer as to whether going through this process makes sense in light of the circumstances of your case.

How Do Emergency Custody Orders Impact Existing Custody Arrangements In New York?

This depends on whether the Judge believes that your emergency application shows valid grounds for changing custody arrangements. If the Judge feels there's enough evidence to warrant it, they can modify, suspend and/or enforce your existing agreement. In other words, your existing arrangement can be wiped out, and a new order can be handed down in light of compelling evidence of abuse.

Are Emergency Custody Orders Temporary Or Permanent?

By their nature, emergency orders are temporary because they serve as a solution to an emergency situation. They will be in effect until a formal trial on the issue. Emergency custody orders can also consider affidavit evidence and hearsay evidence, types of evidence that cannot be admitted at trial.

At trial, you and the other parent will submit your respective evidence and testimony, and a more permanent ruling will be handed down by the Judge.

CHAPTER 14

TOP 7 TIPS FOR CREATING A CHILD VISITATION SCHEDULE

How Can I Ensure The Visitation Schedule Is In The Best Interest Of My Child?

A visitation schedule will vary greatly depending on the age of your child. A very young child will likely have a more flexible schedule than a child in school and involved in sports. A good visitation schedule should consider the needs and activities of your child, their school schedule, and the distance and availability of each parent.

Less disruption is going to be best for your child. A visitation schedule when your child is school-age also factors in your child's friendships, favorite activities, favorite places, and maturity level. Be sure to work with your attorney and with the other party to consider all these factors as amiably and thoughtfully as possible.

How Can I Accommodate Both Of Our Work Schedules In The Visitation Plan?

This depends on what those schedules are. Ideally, your child will spend more time with their parents than with a babysitter or in an afterschool program. I have seen some agreements where even though a child slept over at his mom's house, his dad would pick the child up and take him to school each morning, allowing the mother to get to work earlier.

Other arrangements might involve parents staying over at the other spouse's home while they worked a late shift so the child would not be alone.

An ideal schedule will really factor in both parents' availability as well as the child's needs and allow that child to spend the maximum amount of time with their parents.

Why Is It Important To Be Flexible With The Visitation Schedules?

Both you and the other party will have unforeseen circumstances which arise in life. There might be a funeral, an illness, or something else may come up. The other party may need to take your child to a special event, such as a wedding, outside of the normal visitation schedule.

Remember: if you're not flexible, the other party won't be flexible, either. Try to remain flexible to benefit yourself, the other party as a parent, and your child as well.

What Roles Do Holidays Play In Visitation Planning?

One should include Holidays in visitation plans, especially major holidays like Christmas, New

Year's and Thanksgiving/Black Friday. You may wish to simply allow whichever parent has the child on that day to celebrate with them, or can arrange plans to celebrate one year with you and the next year with the other party.

Include provisions for weddings, funerals, and other events that may come up. Covering these situations in the parenting plan allows you to bring the issue before a Judge if the other party becomes inflexible, not allowing your child to attend a wedding, for example.

What Are The Common Mistakes To Avoid When Creating A Visitation Schedule?

Make sure your visitation schedule is not leaving out holidays, breaks, and vacations. Determine how year-by-year holiday scheduling will work to make sure your plans are enforceable in the long term. For example, many parents' alternate holidays by the year or agree that Thanksgiving will always be with Dad while Christmas will always be with Mom.

What happens if Dad was meant to watch the child but gets called in to work? Can the child stay with his fiancé or with a babysitter (or should the other parent have a "right of 1st refusal")? Are there provisions for uninterrupted private phone time or video calls when the child is with the other parent?

What happens if the child has an activity on the non-custodial parent's access-time? Are they obligated to bring the child? Pick-up the child at the end?

Should there be a grace period regarding how late the non-custodial parent can pick-up the child before a visit is deemed cancelled?

Making sure all these things are worded meaningfully and clearly in the agreement will be vital.

How Do I Handle Missed Visitation Appointments And Make Up Time?

Your visitation agreement should have a provision for time to be made up if one party misses a visit through no fault of their own. For example, if the non-custodial parent misses a visit because of illness or an emergency at work. How are you going to communicate when emergencies arise? Be sure to include how and when that make-up time will happen. The more detailed and comprehensive these provisions are, the better.

What Should One Expect During The Court Approval Process For The Visitation Schedule?

If you and the other party reach a settlement with regard to visitation, the court will almost invariably sign off on that settlement. If you and the other party cannot reach a settlement, then you will have to proceed to trial and have a Judge decide the visitation schedule.

As a result, it is much better to work something out amicably with the other party which considers your respective schedules as well as the well-being and rights of your child. A seasoned family law attorney can help guide you through that process and work meaningfully with the other parent.

CHAPTER 15

CO-PARENTING COMMUNICATION: 3 WAYS TO BUILD A HEALTHY RELATIONSHIP FOR THE SAKE OF YOUR CHILDREN

Effective co-parenting communication is crucial for maintaining a stable and nurturing environment for children after a separation or divorce. Building a healthy relationship with your co-parent can significantly impact your children's well-being and development. Here, we'll explore three essential things you can do to foster constructive and positive communication between you and your co-parent.

Use A Parenting App

Using a parenting app such as Our Family Wizard or Talking Parents may seem like overly simplistic and unnecessarily costly advice if you've never used one before, but once you start, you'll likely wonder why you didn't start using it sooner.

These apps help organize communication by topic, making it easier to manage and refer back to specific discussions. This is particularly useful if disputes arise, as the communication is clearly documented and easily accessible.

Unlike free text or email, it's much easier to ensure that communication is streamlined and topics are kept separate, which is invaluable during disputes. This helps avoid the confusion of sifting through unrelated messages and ensures clarity while saving considerable amounts of time. These apps provide a structured format that can be presented to lawyers or judges if necessary, avoiding the hassle of printing and organizing numerous pages of texts and emails[13].

Engage A Parenting Coordinator

A parenting coordinator is similar to a mediator, helping resolve smaller disputes between co-parents. This can be particularly beneficial during a divorce case or after it has been resolved, addressing issues that don't require legal intervention but still need resolution.

A neutral, experienced professional can help you and your co-parent come to an agreement on various issues without the need to hire lawyers or go to court. This is cost-effective and far less stressful. Parenting coordinators can help resolve everyday disagreements, such as activity choices for children, without escalating to legal battles, saving time and resources.

---

[13] Unsure of the advantages of using such an App versus e-mail/text? Checkout this helpful article: https://www.ourfamilywizard.com/blog/top-5-reasons-use-co-parenting-app

Take A Joint Parenting Skills And Communication Course

There are both online and in-person courses available that focus on improving parenting skills and communication[14]. Taking these courses together can help ensure both you and your co-parent are on the same page regarding parenting strategies and communication methods. It will prepare you and your co-parent to handle conflicts both constructively and cooperatively.

If there are existing communication issues, joint therapy with a family therapist can be beneficial, helping build effective communication skills and address any underlying issues. Ensure the therapist you're considering has experience with family dynamics, especially in the context of divorce. Interview potential therapists as you vet their qualifications and experience.

---

[14] https://ww2.nycourts.gov/ip/parent-ed/index.shtml

Some Additional Tips

- **Regular Check-ins:** If possible, schedule regular check-ins with your co-parent to discuss any issues or concerns regarding the children. Consistent communication can prevent misunderstandings and will go far in building trust where there might not be much.
- **Set Boundaries:** Establish clear boundaries and expectations for communication and co-parenting responsibilities. Respect each other's roles and work together for the well-being of your children.
- **Stay Child-Focused:** As difficult as it may be at times, always prioritize the needs and well-being of your children. Keeping the focus on them will help maintain a collaborative and supportive relationship between you and your co-parent.

CHAPTER 16

Top 10 Legal Options If Your Ex Won't Let You See Your Children

How Does New York Law Protect My Right To Spend Time With My Kids If I Don't Have Custody?

New York law states you need to file for custody immediately. Generally speaking, unmarried persons file a petition in family court, and married persons file a divorce proceeding. If there's an urgent issue in the divorce proceeding, you must file an order to show cause.

It's similar in Family Court: You and your attorney can file an order to show cause because that somewhat expedites your case[15]. If there are access issues, such as the other party not allowing overnight visitation or you are denied adequate parental access you feel you're entitled to, file that order to show cause. Get it in front of the Judge.

Some counties do have court rules regarding the filing of motions. For instance, in Westchester, they require that you file a pre-motion conference letter before you file a motion unless there's an absolute emergency (such as abuse or neglect).

Get that issue before a Judge and have the Judge rule as soon as possible. That's the number one

---

15 https://www.nycourts.gov/LegacyPDFS/FORMS/familycourt/pdfs/gf-1.pdf

priority, especially if you and the other party are separated or if your spouse has taken your kids away.

Can I Change The Custody Agreement If My Ex Prevents Me From Seeing My Kids?

It principally depends on the extent. If the agreement / order says you're to get your kids Friday at six o'clock and your spouse is delivering the kids Friday at seven o'clock, that's a technical violation of the order. If you document it well and it's not rectified, that's worth filing for enforcement.

However, if that's the only thing you have in your favor, it's not likely the Judge is going to switch custody simply because the other party is delivering your children an hour late.

The Judge considers several different factors in a custody determination. Be prepared to present evidence and testimony on each of those factors in your favor and evidence against the other party on those same factors. If you're not ready to do that, your application is not challenging custody so much as enforcing parental access.

What Can I Do If My Child Refuses To Visit Me Because My Ex Is Influencing Them?

Navigating this issue can be difficult and requires great legal care. Is it your child refusing to visit you on their own, or is the other party influencing your child to fear or resent you? If the latter is true, a concept known as parental alienation might be going on.

Attempt to communicate with the custodial parent again. It could be that they're influencing the child, but they don't even realize they're doing so. It may not be a conscious decision. In some cases, bringing that to their attention will help the situation.

You can also offer family counseling or counseling with the child to see what the custodial parent says. Either way, you'll lose nothing by trying to get the child into therapy and talk issues out.

If the custodial parent says, "No, I'm not going to do that for the child," then this is fodder for later litigation in front of a Judge. In such a case, you can tell the Judge:

"I brought my concerns to the custodial parent's attention. They shut my concerns down. I offered to get all of us or our child into therapy. My ex shut that down, too. I'm at a point of last resort before you. I need you to rule on what's happening."

Can I Ask For Extra Time With My Kids If My Ex Doesn't Let Me See Them During My Scheduled Visits?

Most of the time, when people make parenting agreements in divorce or family court, the agreement sets up a minimum baseline of parental access. It doesn't necessarily mean you can't get more. You can request more time.

If the other parent says no, and you have a parenting agreement or order, you have to go back to court at that point. There is no self-help in parental access, especially if you have an order setting forth a schedule.

If your ex has the child in their custody on weekdays and you get every other weekend, you can't (of your own volition) pop up at your child's school on Wednesday and tell them, "You're coming with me tonight."

It's technically illegal for you to do that. Your ex could call the police, file for an order of protection, and/or file for violation of the access agreement/order. There are better ways to go.

If any of the following are true, get the issue in front of the Judge:

- The custody agreement is several years old
- Times or the situation have changed
- The child is older
- The child wants some more access time with the non-custodial parent
- You want more time

How Can I Prove That My Ex Is Violating My Visitation Rights?

It depends on how your ex-spouse is violating your visitation rights. Most people are advised to use parenting apps like OurFamilyWizard, TalkingParents or 2Houses. Those are the standard apps people use. Whether you use those apps or email communication, document every step of the way what the violation was.

If you're supposed to pick up the children at five o'clock on Friday and your ex refuses to produce the children until eight o'clock or doesn't produce them at all, document that. Notify your ex that you were at the pickup location at five o'clock on Friday, and he or she wasn't there. This communication will be confirmation.

Be specific in your documented communication with the other party. For example, you could type: "I later called you to find out where you were, and you merely stated you were on your way, but then you did not show up until three hours later. Please be advised this appears to be a violation of our agreement. Please be on time from now on."

This saved communication keeps a running record of (a) you documenting the violation and (b) your attempts to rectify the situation. Any Judge will look at you cross-eyed if there are multiple violations and you're running back to court without attempting to rectify the situation.

Indeed, some parenting agreements require you to send out a "default notice letter," putting the other side on formal notice of their alleged violation before you do anything. If you attempt to rectify the situation and it can't be remedied, file your application in Family Court.

How Do Courts Usually Handle Cases Where One Parent Denies Visitation For No Good Reason?

The court can take various actions if the other party is denying visitation for no good reason. The court can order makeup time if they feel the custodial parent failed to satisfy the Judge's determination whether they had a good reason to withhold visitation. That order is likely the number one thing the Judge will do.

The Judge also has the power to order sanctions. That can be a fine paid to the state or a counsel fee reimbursement. The fine can be anywhere from several hundred to several thousand dollars as a financial sanction against the custodial parent.

Another action the Family Court or Supreme Court can take on an enforcement application is to order some level of probation or a pickup / drop-off site monitor paid for by the custodial parent. That's not available in every county because they may not have the facilities.

In extreme cases, the Judge can order incarceration or suspend a sentence. The suspension of the sentence could be based on compliance with the visitation schedule. For example, the Judge might say, "I'm going to order this parent to produce themselves to jail on alternate weekends at six o'clock on Friday, but I'll suspend that sentence so long as they comply with scheduled visits. The minute I hear through a written application that this parent has violated any visit, that sentence will be invoked."

The Judge can also order a switch of custody. Generally speaking, the Judge will not switch custody without a full custody hearing. They will consider the violation as a factor in switching custody. The Judge still goes through all the custody factors to decide that a custody switch is in the child's best interest.

Can Mediation Fix The Issue If My Ex Keeps Blocking My Visits With My Kids?

Often, if there's a historical problem with parental access, the recommendation is to involve a parenting coordinator or general mediator. Parenting coordinators are better suited for the task because they have specific expertise in custody and visitation compared to a general mediator.

Suppose parental access has historically been a problem. You can have agreements saying if the parenting coordinator recommends a course of action, and the custodial parent refuses to abide by the recommendation, then that results in a presumptive award of counsel fees to the other side (should they have to bring litigation).

You can craft those sanctions into your parenting agreements or ask the Judge to order them.

The Judge can't ultimately defer to the recommendation of the parenting coordinator, at least in downstate courts. Still, a Judge can consider the custodial parent's refusal to abide by the parenting coordinator's recommendations. Mediation can help in some cases. In others, you have to litigate the issue.

Am I Allowed To Stop Paying Child Support If My Ex Won't Let Me See The Kids?

If there's an order in place for you to pay child support, you would violate the order if you ceased payments. Two wrongs don't make a right. In theory, if your ex is violating visits and you're violating a child support order, the top penalty for each violation is you both go to jail. Presumably, neither of you would want that situation.

Your remedy if your visitation is being violated is to take the issue to court. If you get a court determination that your ex violated your visitation, you could take that back to child support court and request some credit off child support based on their intentional violation of your visitation rights. These are factors the court can consider when modifying child support.

Even when you don't have a court order, it is never a good look to the Judge if your response is, "I'm just not going to pay child support because I'm not seeing the child."

In the Judge's mind, child support is meant to cover the child's portion of housing, utilities, and food. If you're not paying child support, it will seem as if you're saying that you don't care whether or not your child has a place to live, lights to do their homework by, or food to eat.

What Steps Can I Take To Avoid Future Problems With Visitation Through Legal Agreements?

The more specific you are in the language, the better. There are bare-bones agreements that say, "Dad picks up at this location at six o'clock and drops off on Sundays at six o'clock." Then, some agreements are 20 or 30 pages long. The more problematic a situation is, the more specific the agreement has to be to address the potential issues which will likely arise.

For example, what happens when school's not in session? What happens in an emergency such as a snow day? How are the emergencies going to be defined, and by whom? What happens if somebody is running late? What happens when special events arise?

Again, the more detail you put into the agreement, the better off you'll be in a high-conflict situation. With your attorney, discuss all the times you've had problems with the other parent so they can better craft language that zeroes in on those particular issues that you've been having.

CHAPTER 17

TOP 8 MISTAKES THAT CAN IMPACT YOUR CHILD'S FUTURE AFTER DIVORCE

How Could My Co-Parenting Behavior Affect My Child As They Grow Up?

Your co-parenting style can affect your child in positive and negative ways. Your child will fare better if you have positive co-parenting behaviors with the other parent. Ultimately, children are a reflection of their parents. If you have positive interactions with the other parent, the child will see that and react positively, even in a separated household.

Many studies suggest children with separated parents fared better in households with positive co-parenting versus the children remaining with an intact family where the parents are hostile to each other[16].

That may seem obvious, but it's not. Many people think if they divorce their spouse or physically separate from the other parent, that will have grave repercussions for the child. Psychological studies suggest otherwise[17].

On the other hand, the more negative and hostile interactions you have with the other parent, the more negatively it will affect the child.

---

16 See Generally: https://www.americanbar.org/products/inv/book/314773830/

17 https://www.psychologytoday.com/us/blog/going-beyond-intelligence/201905/should-you-stay-together-only-the-kids

In extreme situations, children can feel caught between their parents and show signs of psychological stress, including:

- Fighting with other students in school
- Acting out with teachers in school
- Cutting behavior (i.e., cutting themselves with a knife)
- Engaging in juvenile delinquency

It's a bad situation to have negative co-parenting behaviors. If you think you and the other parent are going down that road, the best advice is to nip that in the bud, get into family counseling and work on your issues. Include your child in counseling sessions and learn how to communicate better. Many times, poor communication is the issue.

What Happens If I Stop My Child From Seeing Their Other Parent?

That depends on why you're stopping the visitation. There are situations where the custodial parent stops the visitation because the non-custodial parent has physically or sexually abused the child.

So, if such extreme situations are occurring, you need to stop the visitation. You also need to get into court ASAP with a modification application - assuming there's already an order to modify in the first place. Don't let the situation persist.

Stopping visits in less extreme situations depends on your reasoning. If you have a good reason for stopping the visit, and this is not a legal issue, you should sit down with the child to discuss why they see the other parent less often. You also want to discuss with the other parent to explain the situation.

If there's an order in place, you don't have the choice to stop the visits. You and your attorney must get the issue before a Judge on a modification application.

How Can Not Having A Set Routine After The Divorce Make Things Harder For My Child?

Everyone thrives with stability, even more so children. Generally, if you have a topsy-turvy schedule, that will be disruptive for a child. The average child needs to know where they will be to plan on getting homework done and know where they're putting their head down at night[18].

The greater the instability in a child's life, the worse that child will fare behaviorally, emotionally and psychologically. Having a set schedule so your child knows weeks in advance where they're going to be is crucial for their well-being.

How Does Dragging My Child Into Custody Disputes Affect Their Mental And Emotional Well-Being?

It depends on the extent to which you involve your children in the dispute and why. Some parents battle in court but keep their children isolated from the litigation. The courts certainly encourage that.

---

18 https://zerotothrive.org/routines-for-kids/#:~:text=Children%20benefit%20from%20relationships%20and,bedtime%20routines%20and%20dinnertime%20routines.

It is recommended your children have minimal involvement with the process, apart from being aware that there's a court proceeding. The court assigns an attorney for your child, but the attorney only interviews them initially and then (usually) checks in with them every two or three months. Otherwise, you and your ex should keep the conflict out of your child's purview.

However, other children are put in the middle of the conflict. The Judge will usually interview your child if you and the other party can't agree on custody. It's what's called an in-camera interview, which means the Judge will interview your child in chambers.

Sometimes, a forensic psychologist will interview your child, perform a psychological evaluation or observe how you and the other party interact with your child[19]. In some cases, there may be

---

19 https://www.psychologytoday.com/us/blog/inside-the-criminal-mind/202012/what-a-forensic-psychologist-does-in-a-child-custody-case

supervised visitation where a social worker is required to observe visitations.

Every case is different, but the more a child gets involved one way or the other with the litigation, the greater the potential for negative repercussions on the child's psychological, emotional or behavioral health.

Should I Make Custody Decisions Based On How My Child Feels In The Moment?

In the custody and visitation realm, it's not up to a child to determine whether they visit with the other parent. Suppose there's an issue where the child expresses reluctance to visit with the other parent. In that case, say, "I hear you. I'll address that with your father / mother." Do so - but leave the child out of it.

When a child says to a custodial parent, "I don't want to visit with Dad this weekend," it's not permissible for the custodial parent to say: "Not a problem. You don't have to[20]."

If there's an agreement or order agreement in place, you would be violating it. Also, you're reinforcing in the child's mind that they have power when they don't. With due respect to children, they don't have the choice of going to school, going for their annual doctor's visit, or going to their biannual dental appointment.

If a child doesn't have that overall level of determination, they also don't have a choice whether they visit with the other parent. If they express reluctance, then it's an adult decision and discussion. If the other parent disagrees with the notion of scaling back the visits, then a Judge must rule on the issue.

---

[20] A variant of this is the parent saying to the child "you do whatever you're comfortable with."

CHAPTER 18

TOP 8 TIPS FOR NEGOTIATING PARENTING TIME DURING HOLIDAYS AND SPECIAL EVENTS

How Can I Request Additional Parenting Time During The Holidays?

The simplest way to request additional parenting time is to start by speaking directly with the other parent. A verbal request can often lead to a quick arrangement, especially if both parties are on good terms and willing to cooperate. For instance, you could ask to have your child on Thanksgiving in exchange for them spending Black Friday with their other parent.

However, if you're unable to reach an agreement, you may need to involve attorneys or a Judge to resolve the matter. If that becomes necessary, it's important to act early. Reach out to your attorney well in advance—especially if your request concerns holidays. Waiting until the last minute could mean the Judge is unavailable or unable to address your request in time.

Keep in mind if the matter goes before a Judge, the outcome may not align with what you or the other parent had hoped. Whenever possible, it's best to work these arrangements out between yourselves to maintain control and avoid potential disappointment. Open communication is often the most efficient and stress-free path to resolving parenting time adjustments.

How Can Mediation Help Resolve Holiday Parenting Disputes?

If you and the other party can't reach a resolution, a mediator can make recommendations and walk you through your various options. There are many different ways of resolving holiday time; because the mediator has years of experience, they can think of creative arrangements that might work better than anything you and the other party could imagine on your own.

For example, you might have your child stay with you on Christmas Eve and have the other parent pick your child up on Christmas morning. In other cases, you could reserve the weekend before or after Christmas, while the other party reserves both Christmas Eve and Christmas Day.

Sometimes, simply sitting down with a neutral, experienced mediator can help guide you toward a solution that works and that everyone is happy with, avoiding the need to get the court involved.

What Happens If My Ex-Spouse Refuses To Follow Our Holiday Schedule?

If your ex-spouse refuses to follow the holiday schedule, the first step is to reach out and calmly let them know you're prepared to pick up or drop off your children as agreed. If they offer excuses, such as the children not feeling well or last-minute plans, make sure to document your objection and propose alternative solutions, like arranging to pick up the children the following day.

Once the holidays are over, contact your attorney to discuss the situation. Keep a record of any missed arrangements, excuses, or lack of cooperation. Your attorney can help bring these violations to the attention of the court, where a Judge may intervene to ensure you receive makeup time with your children. It's important to stay proactive in addressing these issues to protect your rights and ensure the schedule is respected.

What Are Common Mistakes To Avoid When Negotiating Holiday Schedules?

It's surprisingly easy to lose track of your holiday schedule or remember the date but not the specific details, like the time or location for pickup or drop-off. To avoid confusion—especially in high-conflict situations—it's essential to establish clear, concrete plans well in advance. For example, if you have custody during Christmas break, decide exactly when and where the transition will happen. Will you pick your children up from school[21], or will the exchange occur at the other parent's house? At what time?

In addition, ensure that special arrangements for events or family visits don't result in lost parenting time. If the agreement allows your children extra time with "significant relatives" during the holidays, make sure those relationships are clearly defined. Does this refer to grandparents? Step-grandparents? Cousins?

---

[21] Remember that if your "normal" pick-up & drop-off is at school, you'll likely need to specify alternate arrangements during Christmas break (for example) as the schools are closed.

The more specific the terms, the fewer opportunities there are for misinterpretation or manipulation.

Vague or loosely worded agreements often lead to unnecessary conflicts and unfair outcomes. To protect your time and ensure everyone is on the same page, make sure your custody arrangements are as detailed and unambiguous as possible.

What Role Does The Child's Preference Play In Holiday Scheduling?

The role your child's preference plays in holiday scheduling largely depends on their age, the family dynamics, and whether a clear agreement has already been established. For younger children, preferences typically don't factor in, as they lack the independence to act on them. However, older teens—such as 16- or 17-year-olds—may enforce their own preferences simply by leaving to spend time with the other parent.

For children around 13-15, their preferences should be given more weight (as compared to middle-school aged children). Ignoring their wishes can put a significant strain on your relationship and create unnecessary conflict by forcing them into situations they don't want to be in.

That said, sticking to pre-arranged plans is sometimes essential, particularly in high-conflict situations where a lack of consistency could lead to parental alienation. Ultimately, every case is unique. While it's generally wise to take an older child's preferences into account, it's equally important to balance their desires with the need to follow established agreements and maintain a cooperative co-parenting relationship.

How Does Long-Distance Parenting Impact Holiday Schedules?

Long-distance parenting can significantly influence holiday schedules, especially when the distance between parents is substantial. For shorter distances, such as between New York City and Connecticut, holiday arrangements may still resemble traditional schedules. However, when one parent lives across the country, like in California, these arrangements require more careful planning.

In such cases, allocating extended blocks of time to each parent often works best. For example, one parent might have the children for Thanksgiving break, while the other takes Christmas break. Alternatively, for longer winter vacations, time can be divided, such as spending the first week of the break with one parent and the second week with the other, with travel on or around Christmas Eve.

These arrangements not only accommodate the logistical challenges of travel but also ensure both parents get meaningful holiday time with their children. The key? Planning ahead and focusing on practical solutions.

How Does Traveling With Children During The Holidays Affect Custody Agreements?

If you arrange long-distance travel, make sure the flight leaves and arrives at a time that's convenient for your child and the other party.

A Christmas Day flight to California will leave in the morning and get to California by the late morning or early afternoon, Pacific Time. Likewise, a flight from California to New York will not only take six hours but will get in late at night due to the Eastern Time Zone being several hours ahead. In high conflict cases, it's advisable to provide an approximate time range (say 10:00a.m.-1:00p.m.) as opposed to a specific pick-up time – to check for flight delays[22].

Check for these variables and for time zone considerations whenever scheduling long-distance travel. Make sure your child is getting enough rest and sleep for their health, age, and school schedule.

---

[22] One may also wish to build-in contingencies for flight cancellations.

CHAPTER 19

HOW TO HANDLE CHILD NEGLECT OR ABUSE ALLEGATIONS IN COURT

Everyone cares about children, but not everyone has the same amount of information or the same perspective. This can sometimes lead to accusations of child abuse or neglect you never would have imagined but need to know how to respond to. This chapter explains what to do if you are accused of child abuse or neglect in New York, including:

- How to respond to and refute allegations of child abuse or neglect.
- What evidence is needed to demonstrate you have a safe environment for your child.
- How to protect your rights when accused during a custody proceeding.

How you respond to a false accusation of child abuse or neglect largely depends on who is making the accusation:

Accusations From a Parent, Relative, Neighbor, Or Friend

If the accusation comes informally from someone like a relative, friend, or neighbor, you don't necessarily need to respond.

However, if the accusations are detailed or come from the other parent, particularly in writing, and seem connected to an upcoming custody battle or modification, it's wise to respond in writing.

Consider explaining your perspective, possibly with the help of an attorney, to protect yourself from potential legal implications.

Accusations From Child Protective Services (CPS)

If Child Protective Services (CPS) is involved, take immediate and serious action. Contact an attorney who can guide you through the process, help you respond appropriately, and protect your rights.

In these situations, having legal support is essential to ensure your responses align with CPS requirements and prevent further complications.

What Should I Do If I Receive A Call Or Letter From Child Services?

If you're contacted by Child Protective Services (CPS) in New York State, or the Administration for Children's Services (ACS) in New York City, and accused of neglect or abuse, take the following steps:

1. **Contact An Attorney Immediately**

Reach out to a family law attorney as soon as possible, ideally before speaking with a caseworker. Even if child services indicate an emergency requiring a same-day visit, try to schedule an emergency, same-day consultation with an attorney. They can inform you of your rights and help you navigate the process.

2. **Understand Your Rights**

In non-emergency situations, you can ask to delay the meeting until you consult with an attorney. If child services deems it an emergency, they have the legal right to check on the child promptly. However, remember you aren't required to make any statements to the caseworker without legal guidance.

3. **Exercise Caution In Communication**

Similar to criminal proceedings, it's advisable to consult with an attorney before discussing any details with child services. Your attorney can guide you on what, if anything, to communicate and ensure your rights are fully protected during the process.

How Do Child Neglect And Abuse Allegations Affect Custody Proceedings?

Mere allegations (without substantiation) of child abuse or neglect typically do not impact custody proceedings unless they lead to an investigation by Child Protective Services (CPS) or the Administration for Children's Services (ACS). Here's how different outcomes can influence custody:

1. **If the CPS or ACS Investigation Finds Evidence**

If an investigation results in an indicated report—meaning CPS or ACS finds a preponderance of evidence of abuse or neglect—these findings may influence custody or visitation.

However, the indicated report itself is not directly admissible in court; nevertheless, a caseworker may testify about their findings during the custody hearing. You should be prepared to object if the other side attempts to introduce the report itself without proper testimony[23].

2. If the Investigation Leads to a Conviction or Court Finding

A criminal conviction or a Family Court decision affirming abuse or neglect would be admissible in custody proceedings. Such findings often prevent the accused parent from obtaining physical custody and may lead to supervised visitation.

3. If the Investigation Finds No Evidence (Unfounded Case)

If CPS or ACS does not substantiate the allegations, the case is considered unfounded. In this case, the allegations may still be raised, but without official findings, it becomes challenging for the accusing parent to prove them convincingly.

---

[23] Under certain circumstances – and with some exceptions, the Court may admit into evidence a "court-ordered report" by CPS. That said, the Court should not consider hearsay statements made within that report.

An attorney can help either side present or counter allegations effectively, ensuring the court considers relevant evidence or dismisses unfounded claims.

In all cases, having legal guidance is crucial to navigate the complexities of custody proceedings and protect your rights.

What Evidence Can I Gather To Refute Child Neglect Or Abuse Allegations?

If you're facing allegations of child neglect or abuse, working with an attorney is essential to effectively counter these claims. Here are the types of evidence that can help you refute specific allegations:

1. **For Physical Abuse Allegations**

- Expert Testimony

A forensic physician can examine the child and/or medical reports and provide a professional assessment, which can be crucial if CPS or ACS has its own experts. Be prepared for this to involve significant costs, as it requires specialized expertise.

- Statements From Involved Adults

Gather letters or statements from teachers, coaches, or childcare providers who can confirm they have never observed signs of abuse or heard any concerning statements from the child. Ultimately these persons will need to testify - and such testimony would usually be insufficient to refute medical evidence of abuse. But your objective at the outset should be to gather as much evidence as possible to take any wind out of CPS' sails.

2. For Sexual Abuse Allegations

- Forensic Evaluations

Similar to physical abuse cases, hiring experts to conduct evaluations and provide testimony can be key to refuting allegations, particularly if CPS or ACS is prepared with its own experts.

3. For Neglect Allegations

- Relevant Documentation

Tailor your evidence to address specific allegations. For instance, if the claim is school absenteeism, gather records of communications with the school, proof of tutoring sessions, or evidence of counseling to show efforts to support the child's education.

- Records Of Actions Taken

If the neglect claim involves unmet medical needs, provide records of appointments, prescriptions, and follow-ups to demonstrate that the child's health was appropriately addressed.

4. **For Domestic Violence Allegations**

- Protective Actions

If you're a victim of domestic violence, document steps you took to shield the child from exposure, such as staying in a shelter or filing for a protective order.

- Counter-Evidence

If you're accused of domestic violence, gather evidence showing that the child was not exposed to any violence. This can include statements from those who've observed the child's behavior or environment.

You should also gather all evidence undercutting the accuser's narrative – this may include evidence of friends or relatives who never heard any complaints of domestic violence, lack of police/medical reports and the possibility of forensic evidence (such as google maps tracking showing one wasn't home at the time of the alleged incident).

5. **Demonstrating A Safe Environment**

- Home Conditions

Photos and videos of your home, showing clean, well-kept living spaces, stocked food supplies, and safe sleeping areas for your child, can directly counter claims of inadequate living conditions.

- Corroborative Testimonies

Contact teachers, counselors, or family friends who can attest to the child's well-being and confirm they have not observed signs of excessive punishment or fear.

Preparing this evidence not only refutes false claims but also demonstrates your commitment to providing a safe and supportive environment for your child, strengthening your defense.

How Can I Ensure My Rights Are Protected During A CPS Investigation?

To protect your rights during a CPS investigation, having the right attorney is critical. Look for an attorney with specific experience in abuse and neglect cases, as not all attorneys are equally skilled in this area. While some attorneys claim to have experience with these cases, it's important to confirm their effectiveness.

To evaluate for yourself how good an attorney is, try to determine:

- What do their Google reviews say?

- What are their objective qualifications?
- What is their caseload like?
- How many actual cases like yours have they handled (don't accept a vague response like "many")

You want someone who will have enough time to devote to your case; the last thing you want is for them to run out of time to be able to devote adequate resources to your defense against child abuse or child neglect accusations.

What Should I Do If The Court Orders A Child Protection Investigation?

How you respond to a child protection investigation depends on whether it targets you or the other parent.

If The Investigation Targets The Other Parent

If CPS is investigating the other parent, the advice is straightforward: cooperate with CPS. Speak with them, answer their questions honestly, and allow them to talk with the children.

If The Investigation Targets You

If the allegations are directed at you, it's important to take action. Follow the same steps above, but also contact an attorney immediately. If a Judge orders an investigation focused on you during a custody or visitation hearing, schedule an appointment with your attorney right away to figure out:

- What's happening,
- How to defend yourself, and
- What to say to the caseworker who will likely visit in the next few days.

An attorney can also advise you on handling false accusations from an ex, especially if they're intended to harm your case[24].

---

[24] For general information, checkout: https://www.wikihow.com/Survive-Allegations-of-Child-Abuse

Can I Pursue Legal Action Against My Ex For Making False Accusations?

Legal action against your ex for false accusations is only possible if you can prove those claims were knowingly false. Simply having the accusations dismissed or unproven, in itself, isn't enough to pursue a lawsuit.

For example, to hold CPS or the police accountable for a false arrest, you would generally need to prove they acted without probable cause. Just showing that the investigation didn't uphold the allegations wouldn't be enough. You'd have to demonstrate they had no valid reason to arrest you in the first place.

The same logic applies in Family Court. If the other parent accuses you of abuse or neglect, a Judge would first need to determine that the accusations were false. Even with this ruling, however, you'd still need to prove in a separate lawsuit that the accuser knowingly and intentionally made those false claims.

The Judge's finding is helpful—but not enough by itself—to meet this burden of proof.

What Should I Expect During A Family Court Hearing On Child Neglect Or Abuse?

If you're facing a court hearing specifically for abuse or neglect—not just allegations within a custody or visitation case—your first appearance will likely be a 1027 hearing. During this hearing, the Judge will assess whether temporary orders are needed. This may include deciding if there's a basis to remove the child from your home.

If your child has already been removed, the Judge will determine whether this should continue or if other orders are necessary. After the hearing, motions can be made to attempt a resolution, but if no agreement is reached, the court will schedule trial dates.

If you don't have an attorney by this point, it's essential to get one immediately to help navigate these proceedings and protect your rights.

It is beyond the scope of this book to provide a detailed explanation of these types of cases or how best to defend oneself. I refer readers to my book "Navigating Your New York Family Court Case" as well as this link for more information: https://familylegalcare.org/guide/child-abuse-and-neglect/.

CHAPTER 20

TOP STRATEGIES FOR NEGOTIATING ALIMONY PAYMENTS

How Can I Determine A Fair Amount For Alimony?

The first step in determining alimony (a/k/a "spousal maintenance") is to factor in both partners' incomes into a maintenance calculator. Many clients find the Joy Rosenthal calculator[25] to be a helpful and accurate tool. While not definitive, it can help give you a good idea of what alimony might be in New York.

This calculator computes presumptive numbers for spousal maintenance and child support. You can lower or raise numbers as you like, and this tool can help you come up with some numbers that are helpful in negotiation.

Many clients propose a number that's anywhere from half to the full amount of this calculated amount based on other facts such as asset distribution, custody, or child support. But once you have this number, it's a helpful figure to use going into negotiations.

Key Factors to Consider When Negotiating Spousal Maintenance

When negotiating spousal maintenance, several statutory factors come into play:

---

25 https://www.joyrosenthal.com/new-york-maintenance-child-support-calculator/

- **Age and Health:** The age and health of both parties.
- **Earning Capacities:** Present or future earning capacities of the parties.
- **Need for Training or Education:** The need of the party requesting maintenance to incur training or education for a future job.
- **Termination of Prior Child Support:** The impact of terminating prior child support awards.
- **Disposition of Assets:** Getting rid of assets or property - or distributing same between the parties.
- **Premarital Household:** The existence of a premarital household.
- **Impact of Domestic Violence:** Acts, such as physically debilitating domestic violence, that have affected the victimized party's ability to earn.
- **Tax Consequences:** Tax consequences of either maintenance, child support and/or asset distribution.

- **Standard of Living:** The standard of living for both parties. Higher standards of living generally command higher spousal maintenance payments.
- **Lost Earning Capacity:** Reduced or lost earning capacity as a result of delaying education or work, such as a spouse who sacrificed college to stay home and raise children.
- **Spousal Contributions:** Contributions of a spouse or parent to the earning potential of the moneyed party, such as staying home with the children to allow the other to grow their business.
- **Other Relevant Factors:** Any other potentially relevant factors, such as egregious misconduct from the moneyed spouse.

Tip: Review All These Factors With Your Attorney

How long you and your spouse have been living separately is also important. It's not uncommon for a spouse to have been living on their own and earning independently, only to request spousal maintenance. This can be contested by an attorney, who can examine the other party's finances to determine an appropriate alimony amount.

All of these factors should be reviewed at length with your attorney to help them get a clear picture of your marriage, the finances of both parties while you were together, and what both parties' finances might look like post-divorce.

I recommend one creates a chart listing both positive & negative facts regarding oneself as to each statutory factor – as well as a separate chart listing positive & negative facts one expects the other side to introduce.

How Can Mediation Help In Alimony Negotiations?

A mediator will sit down with you and your spouse after reviewing both of your financial statements. The mediator will come up with a presumptive number for alimony and discuss issues such as your expected budget for living expenses after divorce, expected asset distribution, and what both parties feel they will need moving forward.

Ideally, the mediator helps you and the other party reach an acceptable middle ground, somewhere between zero and the presumptive number. This is where your calculated alimony figure can potentially come in handy, along with guidance and representation from your attorney.

Alimony Laws Specific To New York

The above-mentioned statutory factors will be important in any New York alimony debate. It's also important to understand that the length of the marriage will play a role in determining alimony. In New York, alimony is paid out for a percentage of the length of the marriage. The presumptive durations are set forth below:

- A marriage lasting less than 15 years is a "short-term marriage." In this case, alimony will be presumptively paid for 15% to 30% of the length of the marriage.

- A marriage lasting between 15 and 20 years will see alimony presumptively paid for 30% to 40% of the duration of the marriage.
- A marriage that lasts more than 20 years will see alimony presumptively paid out for 35% to 50% of the length of the marriage.

If you are presently out of work or have reduced your earnings as of late, be sure to keep up the search for a job that will match or be close to your previous earnings. Similarly, if your spouse is seeking maintenance, consider allowing a vocational expert to investigate your former spouse's job search.

Be sure to go over all of the above factors with your attorney to ensure a more fair and understandable alimony settlement.

How Do I Document Financial Needs And Expenses So It's Done Accurately?

Expenses can be documented very easily with programs like Quicken or QuickBooks. This can help supplement other documents, such as credit card statements, bank statements, and tax returns.

So much of our financial lives are digital now, in the form of credit or debit, but a spreadsheet can still be a helpful way to demonstrate you are taking the documentation of your finances seriously and accounting for everything with care.

A spreadsheet is also more helpful for a Judge than dozens (or hundreds) of pages of separate documentation. The courts will also require a "statement of net worth" to be filled out documenting your assets and finances. Having accurate records will make these forms far simpler to fill out when the time comes.

What Are The Benefits Of Negotiating Lump Sum Alimony Payments?

Upfront maintenance in the form of a lump sum may be helpful if you have considerable assets and your spouse is looking to move out and purchase a home or a condo immediately. This will require a considerable down payment, and giving that amount upfront may be preferable to paying out presumptive amounts over several years.

This can allow you to pay, for example, $20,000 at once instead of $36,000 over three years. This can help save you money in the long run, as well as get the other party the accommodations they need far sooner.

Are There Any Downsides In Negotiating A Lump Sum Alimony Payment?

While spousal maintenance is not taxable at the federal level, it is still taxable at the State level. If you do get a lump sum in alimony from a spouse, sit down with an accountant to determine if this arrangement will make sense from a fiscal standpoint.

It may ultimately make more sense for you to receive payments over time, especially as you will still owe New York taxes on any alimony amount you receive.

Some spouses find it simpler to take in smaller amounts of alimony to avoid higher taxes. This opportunity to avoid higher taxation can be a helpful negotiating point in determining asset distribution and payments. If you anticipate receiving alimony payments, talking to a financial planner[26] can also help you decide whether to accept a lump sum or take those payments over time.

What Are The Risks Of Not Having A Clear And Detailed Alimony Agreement?

Failing to establish a clear and detailed alimony (a/k/a maintenance) agreement can lead to significant issues and disagreements in the future. When an alimony plan is vague or lacks specificity, it increases the likelihood of disputes and makes it less likely a Judge will approve the arrangement.

One of the simplest and most effective ways to avoid future conflicts is to clearly specify the amount of alimony to be paid. For example, agreeing on a fixed amount, such as $5,000 per month, leaves little room

---

[26] Consider a Certified Divorce Financial Analyst: https://institutedfa.com/

for interpretation and reduces the chances of disputes later on.

However, it's also essential to consider potential future changes in the financial circumstances of either party. What happens if the recipient's earnings decrease, or conversely, if they suddenly begin earning a substantial income, such as $500,000 a year? In such cases, does the original alimony amount still make sense?

One may consider inserting clauses checking for maintenance modification scenarios, such as financial hardship, or changes of income which exceed 15%.

Discuss these scenarios with your attorney to ensure that your alimony agreement addresses how changes in circumstances will be handled.

Chapter 22

How To Compromise And Avoid Conflict During A Divorce

How Can I Compromise During Conflict In My Divorce?

Mediation is a common way for couples to compromise with one another during a complicated divorce. At least 50% of the time, the mediation process is successful and helps both parties move through the proceedings with less tension[27]. You could search for a divorce mediator online but, in New York State, many people are referred to a mediator by their attorney or the Court.

Mediators typically meet with you and your spouse for one to three sessions to attempt to resolve your divorce or family law issue. Using a mediator can save you time and money over each party hiring their own lawyer[28], but it's best to choose mediation only if you're confident your spouse will negotiate in good faith and work with you.

It's also important for both you and your spouse to understand that compromise and give-and-take will

---

[27] Indeed, some studies indicate the mediation success rate may be as high as 70-80% - https://www.americanbar.org/groups/public_education/resources/law_related_education_network/how_courts_work/mediation_advantages/

[28] This article linked to a 1988 study showing that mediation saved parties nearly $700 - https://www.researchgate.net/publication/230238997_Divorce_Mediation_Outcome_Research_A_Meta-Analysis. In 2025 dollars, this would be nearly $2,000.

be necessary on both sides. The list of things you will likely need to compromise on can include:

- Property and asset distribution
- Debt distribution
- Child support
- Alimony
- Custody and visitation rights
- And more…

But this doesn't mean each and every issue needs to be handled separately during mediation. For example, it may happen that you or your spouse let go of hard stances in your parenting time agreement in exchange for paying less in child support.

This process could also take the form of acknowledging that you earn enough to take care of yourself and thus letting go of alimony rights. This sacrifice can then help you leverage negotiations in your benefit elsewhere and make the process less tense and fairer for both sides.

You can also find ways to compromise on property and asset distribution. You may find yourself wanting to keep a house, while the other party would like to sell. Compromise in this situation may mean that the sale of the house is delayed until a child turns 18, or your spouse receives a little bit more in alimony payment as the home sale is delayed. Alternatively, you could agree to pay all of the remaining mortgage, allowing you to keep the home while freeing the other party from that debt.

Should a house be sold, you may also want to compromise on the distribution of the sale proceeds, depending on what improvements were made, who paid most of the mortgage, who has custody of a child, and other factors. These compromises and negotiations could also include increased visitation rights, greater or lesser alimony pay, or changes to custody agreements.

As you begin the journey of working to resolve roadblocks with the other party, it's important that you realistically consider what their litigation position would be and what they would be willing to settle for.

Understand what their position and offers are from the beginning and be willing to work from that point. This can help both you and your spouse move forward with less conflict and come to arrangements both faster and more efficiently.

CHAPTER 23

COPING STRATEGIES IN A NEW YORK DIVORCE: BEST 5 WAYS TO HANDLE STRESS AND EMOTIONAL CHALLENGES

Divorce is an undeniably challenging experience, often marked by intense emotional turmoil, overwhelming legal complexities, and significant life changes. Navigating this difficult journey can feel unbearable, but there are ways to ease the transition.

My goal here is to provide you with some practical advice and support if you're going through a divorce. The five key pieces of advice I unpack range from focusing on self-care to managing legal aspects efficiently, but they are all designed to help you find stability and hope during the incredibly tumultuous time you're either about to start or already find yourself trudging through.

1. Connect With A Therapist

Divorce is statistically one of the most stressful events in a person's life. Engaging with a therapist can help you manage the stress you'll likely experience. If you already have a mild mental illness, it's only exacerbated by the stress of a divorce case.

If you happen to already be in therapy, let your therapist know about your situation. They may adjust your treatment plan, increasing session frequency or modifying medication if necessary. Do your best to fight against any stigma you may have about therapy. Many people view seeing a therapist as a negative thing, but it shouldn't be, especially in contested custody or visitation matters.

In the context of your divorce case or any related issues, such as custody or visitation, being in therapy (in itself) will have no bearing on the outcome. A Judge or jury won't view you in a negative light, for example, if you're seeing a therapist - only being diagnosed with something that inhibits your ability to care for your children would.

2. **Monitor And Support Your Children**

Just like adults, children also experience stress during a divorce. If your children are already in therapy, inform their therapist about the divorce to see if additional support will be needed. If they are not in therapy, watch for signs of stress, such as acting out, inattentiveness, or a decline in school performance. Regularly check in with your children's teachers and counselors to monitor their well-being and address any issues promptly.

3. **Consult With An Attorney Early**

Consulting with an attorney before initiating a divorce will help you understand the legal process and prepare for what lies ahead. This can dramatically reduce anxiety and prevent unpleasant surprises from popping up later in the process. Many attorneys offer free resources such as eBooks, blogs or discounted initial consultations. Use these to educate yourself about the divorce process as a supplement to directly meeting with an attorney.

4. **Hire A Specialized Attorney**

Hiring an attorney at the earliest possible stage of your divorce process is critical for so many reasons. Many mistakenly believe they can handle their divorce on their own, often thinking:

- I'm intelligent; I can do this.
- I do my own taxes, so why can't I do my own divorce?
- I'm an attorney; I know the law. I don't need an attorney to represent me.

True as these things may seem to be, it's still absolutely essential to hire a good attorney, especially one who has a specialty in divorce law. They'll be able to guide you through gathering documents, planning for contested issues, and navigating court proceedings. More than this, they will provide a roadmap for your case, outlining points of intersection between the strategy you've adopted and the steps of the legal process. Bottom-line: if you wouldn't perform surgery on yourself, don't represent yourself.

5. **Maintain Regular Communication With Your Attorney**

Before each court date, have a check-in with your attorney to understand what to expect and prepare any necessary documents or arguments. Likewise, after each court appearance, schedule a debrief with your attorney to clarify any confusion, understand the outcomes, and plan the next steps. This communication reduces anxiety and keeps you informed about your case's progress.

CHAPTER 24

HEALING AND GROWTH: 5 SELF-CARE SUGGESTIONS FOR MOVING FORWARD AFTER DIVORCE

Healing and personal growth are integral parts of moving forward after a divorce, making for a period of profound transformation and a renewed sense of self. Although they're not legal advice, strictly speaking, I'll break down five practical self-care suggestions I've gathered over the years of helping clients so you can effectively navigate this emotional journey.

1. **Exercise**

You might be scratching your head at this point, but hear me out. Exercise is an excellent stress reliever. It releases endorphins, which help improve mood and reduce anxiety.

If you haven't been exercising, start now. This could be a home routine, joining a gym, or hiring a personal trainer for motivation. No matter where you do it, the important thing is to start. Finding an activity you enjoy, whether it's running, yoga, cycling, or any other form of physical activity, will help you stick with it.

2. **Get Good Sleep**

Proper sleep is foundational to good mental and physical health. A lack of sleep will exacerbate stress and affect your overall well-being. Here are some tips to get better sleep:

- Invest in a comfortable mattress and pillows that support your sleep position.
- Create a relaxing bedtime routine, such as reading, meditating, or taking a warm bath.

- Use an eye mask or blackout curtains to block out light and earplugs if noise is a particular issue.
- Incorporate yoga & meditation. Doing so can improve the quality of your sleep, namely by making it easier to fall asleep and stay asleep throughout the night.

3. Maintain A Healthy Diet

Good, nutritious diets have been shown to positively affect mood and energy levels[29]. On the other hand, poor eating habits contribute to stress. Cut out junk food, sugary snacks, sodas, and excessive amounts of alcohol. Focus on balanced meals with plenty of fruits, vegetables, lean proteins, and whole grains.

---

[29] "There's clear medical evidence that nutrition affects our emotional well-being and can reduce the risk of anxiety." https://health.clevelandclinic.org/eat-these-foods-to-reduce-stress-and-anxiety

Although this may be especially difficult, I highly recommend reducing alcohol intake to one drink per day, if at all. Alcohol can worsen stress and should not be used as a coping mechanism, despite what might be a common practice in our society.

4. **Consider Therapy**

Therapy can provide a safe space to process emotions and develop coping strategies.

If you're not already in therapy, consider starting. Divorce is a significant life stressor, and professional support can truly be invaluable. If you are in therapy, discuss increasing session frequency or adjusting medications with your therapist based on your needs. Cognitive-behavioral therapy, in particular, can be considerably effective for managing stress and anxiety.

5. **Explore Mindfulness**

Mindfulness might come off as the latest buzzword, but there's a lot more to it than what may meet the eye. It can help you stay present and reduce stress by cultivating a calm, organized mind. If you're open to it, consider:

- Engaging in daily meditation or deep-breathing exercises to help center yourself.
- Keeping a daily diary to organize your thoughts and plan your days effectively.
- Being intentional about planning simple things, like allowing extra time for travel to avoid rushing. This can reduce many smaller daily stressors that would otherwise snowball throughout your day.
- Exploring cognitive-behavioral techniques with a therapist to develop structured plans for managing stress, if necessary.

The main point here is to take time each day to check in with yourself emotionally and mentally.

CHAPTER 25

DATING AFTER DIVORCE: 5 WAYS TO EXPLORE NEW RELATIONSHIPS AND PRIORITIZE SELF-DISCOVERY

Reentering the dating scene after a divorce can be both exciting and intimidating, offering a chance to explore new relationships while also fostering self-discovery. Navigating this new chapter requires a balance of openness to new experiences and a focus on personal growth.

In this chapter, I'll discuss five key pieces of advice I've gathered from working with clients over the course of my career. My drive here is to help you confidently and thoughtfully approach dating after divorce.

1. **Exercise Caution When Introducing A New Partner To Your Children**

Introducing a significant other to your children can be a sensitive issue for both your children and their other parent. Be mindful of how you structure these introductions and relationships.

As you draw closer to the point in the relationship where you feel it appropriate to introduce your new partner to your children, engage in open discussions with your co-parent about specifically how and when to introduce them to your children.

Why? Doing so helps maintain a respectful co-parenting relationship and considers the emotional well-being of your children. Although the other parent doesn't have veto power, the upside of taking their feelings into account to ensure smooth co-parenting far outweighs the downside.

2. **Understand The Legal Implications Of Dating During A Divorce**

Technically, you are still married until the divorce is finalized by a Judge, and in the State of New York, engaging in sexual relations before a divorce is finalized is considered adultery.

Though the Penal Law was amended in November, 2024 to specify that adultery is no longer a crime in New York, this doesn't mean your ex won't try to raise the issue in the divorce case – particularly if custody or visitation is an issue.

3. **Evaluate The Suitability Of Your Partner**

This is true of anyone, even those not dating after a divorce, but it still nevertheless needs to be said considering how it's even more relevant in your situation: Be cautious about who you date, especially if they have a history of violent or criminal behavior.

Verify any claims made by your new partner, especially if they have had issues with child welfare or have a criminal record. Ensuring your new partner is trustworthy and safe is vital for the well-being of your children. Avoid taking risks based on the partner's claims without thorough verification. You don't necessarily have to police them, but you just want to be mindful of these sorts of things. Newly divorced people date people they shouldn't far more often than you might think.

4. **Maintain Boundaries Between Your Ex-Spouse And New Partner**

If you have ongoing financial ties with your ex-spouse, such as property distribution or spousal maintenance, keep your new partner away from these matters. Interaction between your ex-spouse and your new partner can lead to unnecessary conflicts.

Maintain clear boundaries so as to prevent these complications from arising. Focus on resolving any outstanding issues with your ex-spouse without the input of your new partner, who likely doesn't have a full understanding of the context or may have an unfounded sense of entitlement to money, for example. If you owe spousal support, there's nothing that can be done about this, and any frustration your new partner may feel as a result can be avoided by having clear boundaries in place from the beginning.

5. Embrace Self-Discovery

If you're divorced, you're free! Take some time to reflect and grow. Focus on understanding your needs, desires, and what you seek in future relationships before rushing into one. Prioritizing self-discovery helps you build a stronger sense of self and make healthier choices in future relationships. It also ensures you enter new relationships with a clear understanding of your own values and boundaries. And don't allow your ex-spouse to dictate who you date or when you do. If you don't have any children with them, move on with your life.

CHAPTER 26

TOP QUESTIONS TO ASK YOUR NEW YORK DIVORCE LAWYER BEFORE YOU FILE

Do I Really Need An Attorney In New York To File For A Divorce?

You do not *need* an attorney to file for a divorce, though it is highly recommended that you at least consult an attorney before proceeding. This is especially true if you have children, assets, property, or the possibility of alimony. It is always best to have a lawyer represent you and your interests.

If you wish to begin the process on your own, New York court's website has uncontested divorce forms that you and your spouse can fill out and submit to the court - if there are no conflicts or disagreements between you. Bear in mind these forms are best for couple who do not have children or assets (even if you both are waiving distribution of assets).

Even so, having an attorney's help is best. Many divorces that seem simple at first can become more complex as the process progresses. A lawyer can also ensure all paperwork is filed correctly and answer any legal, personal, and financial questions that arise along the way.

What Are The Grounds For Divorce In New York, And How Do They Apply To My Case?

In New York, the grounds for divorce include "no-fault," also known as "irretrievable breakdown" or "irreconcilable differences."

This simply means you feel your marital relationship has broken down, cannot be fixed, and should be legally ended. This is the ground under which

99.9% of divorces in New York are filed these days, no matter the circumstances of the marriage's ending.

Other grounds include cruel and inhuman treatment, abandonment, or a marriage's initial invalidity, known as annulment.

Is There A Waiting Period For A Divorce In New York?

The courts require that the breakdown of the marriage occur within the last six months, though this can sometimes be fluid, and the courts do not strictly police this time period.

You will simply have to sign a sworn document saying you believe your marriage has broken down irretrievably for at least six months, and this allows you to file.

What Are My Legal Options If My Spouse Doesn't Want To Get Divorced?

If you anticipate your spouse will object to the divorce, it is best to ensure they are served with a summons via a licensed process server. After they are served, they have 20 days to answer the summons.

If they do, this allows them to object to the grounds and argue there has not been an irretrievable breakdown of the marriage. Should that happen, the courts could still hold a grounds trial to determine the validity of the no-fault basis for divorce, though this is quite rare.

Realistically, it is very difficult to argue against a no-fault divorce. If you simply do not want to be married to your spouse and you feel the marriage has broken down beyond repair, a court is almost certain to agree with you and grant you a divorce.

How Long Does The Divorce Process Typically Take In New York?

This depends on whether your divorce is contested or uncontested and where your case is filed. For example, in Westchester, New York, your no-fault, uncontested divorce should take about three to six months. A contested divorce will take an average of 12 to 18 months to go through a full trial.

In the Bronx, however, an uncontested divorce can take six to ten months, while a contested divorce can take 12 to 24 months. This is simply due to the number of available Judges and staffing from one court to another and the sheer population difference in certain towns and boroughs.

What Is The Cost Of Filing For Divorce, And What Are The Potential Legal Fees?

As of September 2024, the court fee to file in New York is $210. Fees may go up over time, so verifying those exact fees on the New York State Courts website is best.

Attorney's fees vary greatly. You could spend as little as a few hundred dollars or as much as tens of thousands of dollars just to hire your attorney. The differences in fees reflect the attorney's experience level, qualifications, where their office is located, their caseloads, and the structure of their practice.

For example, an attorney who recently graduated law school will charge far less than someone with 20 or 30 years of experience. Likewise, an attorney with larger caseloads of 150 or more will charge far less than an attorney with 50 to 70 cases. Larger caseloads mean less time to spend on your case and lower fees, while smaller caseloads can allow you more dedicated attention with a higher bill.

How Should I Prepare For Divorce As A Parent?

Sit down with an attorney and talk about your situation, the background of your marriage, your child's situation, and your hopes for your future with your child. Before the divorce occurs, keeping records can be an incredibly helpful way to prepare.

Keep a dated journal of your daily interactions with your child with regard to picking them up from school, childcare, and your involvement in their lives versus your spouse's involvement.

Preserve emails, text messages, and social media messages from the other parent, as well. If you have audio recordings of conversations with your spouse, these can also be quite helpful. You should also checkout the downloadable books on my website: www.blivenlaw.net

What Financial Information Should I Prepare Before A Divorce?

Get ahold of all documents related to your finances, major purchases, real estate transactions, and transfers of money. This can help verify whether assets are jointly held or solely your own, something helpful to establish in the division of assets. Photocopy all checks written and get copies of all statements.

Similarly, it's important to determine which portion of your retirement accounts are premarital for you to retain that amount after divorce. Get statements from your 401k or deferred compensation plan to show how much money you had in these accounts at the time you were married.

You will also likely have to fill out a "net worth statement" - so getting together documentation related to bank accounts, assets, and liabilities will be important. Should your divorce be contested, you will need to provide this documentation for (at least) the last three years, so it's best to get started on this as soon as possible.

In fact, my website has a free, downloadable eBook called "Navigating Your New York Contested Divorce Case." Within that eBook, I've included a list of documents to start getting together if your case is contested.

How Will The Divorce Affect My Taxes / Are There Any Tax Benefits?

This depends on the issue and the circumstances of your divorce. For example, if alimony (a/k/a spousal maintenance) is paid, it is deductible to the payer and included as income for the receiver under New York State tax law.

Talk with your spouse as to whether you'd like to file your taxes jointly one last time for the year that you file for divorce. Exceptions to this include if your spouse is especially violent, controlling, or financially abusive. If so, have a conversation with an accountant as to what filing situation makes the most sense for you financially.

You will also want to discuss tax deductions or which spouse gets to claim your children as dependents on their tax returns. Generally, this is something the custodial parent does, though your unique custodial situation will require a conversation of its own during negotiations. In other cases, a court can make that decision for you.

How Does Hiring A Divorce Attorney In New York Make The Process Easier For Me?

An attorney will be able to guide you through a New York divorce far better than you could ever manage on your own. Your attorney will know the law and can marshal proper arguments to make on your behalf to a Judge.

No matter how intelligent you are, how educated you are, or how respected you are in your field, you will need a divorce attorney. I've seen highly intelligent clients with multiple PhDs who fired their attorney, assumed they could handle the divorce on their own, and were utterly creamed by the Divorce Judge.

CHAPTER 27

THE BEST TIPS FOR CHOOSING THE RIGHT DIVORCE ATTORNEY IN NEW YORK

What Are Some Of The Qualities I Should Look For In A Divorce Attorney?

When you are looking for a divorce attorney, experience will always be the quality you should consider first and foremost. While this is not always the case, more experience generally means that an attorney is better suited to handle your case. For this reason, someone with 20 or 30 years of experience will be far more prepared to assist you than someone with one or two years of experience.

It would also be wise to consider working with an attorney who is experienced in working on behalf of clients with a similar background to you. For instance, if you earn a modest income, it may not be in your best interest to work with a lawyer who caters to high-income clients (or vice versa).

Aside from experience, reviews are also important to consider when looking for an attorney. Reviews should not make or break your decision, but it can be very helpful to look at both positive *and negative* reviews on sites like Avvo and Google. This way, you can address any concerns related to negative reviews with your attorney directly. If your attorney responds defensively to your concerns, this could raise a red flag for continuing to work with them.

Another thing to look for in your potential attorney is objective qualifications. Objective qualifications are generally issued by major legal publishers such as Martindale-Hubbell and Thomson Reuters to rate attorneys based on their legal ability, ethical standards, and performance history. If an attorney has close to a 10.0 rating on Avvo, rated a "Super Lawyer" on Thomson Reuters, or has an "AV" rating from Martindale Hubbell, this generally rates them toward the top of the field.

If your potential lawyer has sub-par ratings through objective qualifications, you, as a prospective client, should wonder why.

Apart From Experience And Reputation, What Else Should I Consider When Choosing A Divorce Attorney?

When you sit down with that attorney, do they look you in the eye? Are they attentive and sympathetic to your situation, or do they seem like they will rush through your case? You can get a lot out of considering how an attorney treats you during your initial consultation.

It is important to consider the caseload of your potential attorney, as you will become a part of it if you choose to work together. Beyond asking what their caseload is, you can also use www.nycourts.gov (& click thru to WebCivil Supreme or WebFamily) to see a particular attorney's caseload when it comes to divorce or family law cases. Several studies have shown that attorneys with a caseload higher than 70 or 80 cases are taking on too much.

When your case goes to court, you want to be sure you are being represented by an attorney who will look out for your best interests. Much like with the caseload, you should speak to your attorney about whether or not other lawyers will be assigned to your case. You'd be surprised by how often people meet with the high-powered, gray-haired Senior Partner at the initial consultation, only to end up having a less-experienced Associate doing the bulk of work on your case. This way, you can avoid any surprises by opening and maintaining lines of communication with everyone who is assigned to your case.

Additionally, you should look into any awards or certifications the attorney may have that could benefit your case. For instance, if your case involves a financial analysis, you would greatly benefit from working with an attorney who holds certified financial litigator status with the American Academy of Certified Financial Litigators. Likewise, are his/her paralegals "Certified Financial Paralegals?" Not all of these qualifications are necessary, but it is important to do your due diligence before hiring a divorce attorney.

How Can I Evaluate The Communication Skills Of An Attorney During An Initial Consultation?

Oftentimes, the events leading up to the consultation (as well as the events that follow) will help you to thoroughly evaluate an attorney's communication skills. For instance, if you notice a pattern of difficulty in getting anyone on the phone, this could be a red flag for poor communication skills. If you find it difficult to get in touch with and receive straight answers from a law firm you are considering working with, you may want to question if they are best suited for your situation. Ask your potential attorney what policy they have in place to ensure consistent updates regarding your case[30].

You can also take into account what happens after your consultation when determining the communication style of a potential attorney. Does the attorney establish a clear timeframe in which you will hear from them? Do they stick to that timeframe and communicate clearly when they follow up with you?

If you fail to hear from a lawyer for several days and have to reach out to *them* after your consultation, this could be a red flag. If you have a consultation with a firm that consistently follows up to ensure you have received any updates and quotes in a timely fashion, this shows dedication to the success of your case.

---

30 Do they copy/blind-copy clients on all e-mails? Do they always send clients notes of their phone conversations or court appearances?

How Can I Gauge An Attorney's High-Conflict Divorce Experience?

In my experience, the best way is simply to ask. For instance, if your assets are worth millions and your income is in the high six figures, you can ask an attorney how many cases of this size they have worked on. While your attorney can not divulge the names of clients they have worked with, they should be able to share how many cases of a similar nature they have worked on before[31].

It is also important to consider how an attorney responds to these questions. If you ask how many cases of a particular nature the lawyer has worked on and they are unable to provide information about the facts of a case, it is possible they have not taken any cases similar to yours.

---

[31] Don't accept "many" as an answer. The attorney may not have a specific number off the top of their head at the initial consult, but they should be able to e-mail you an approximate number after double-checking their past cases after the consult.

What Red Flags Should I Be Aware Of When Looking For A Divorce Attorney?

Two prominent red flags easily researched online are negative reviews and the lack of any published articles or books in their field. Ideally, the lawyer you choose to represent you should have a history of positive reviews from clients and a series of reputable publications. Another red flag to look out for is an ultra-high caseload.

There are a number of attorneys in New York who are public defenders in addition to being private attorneys, commonly referred to as 18B lawyers. 18B lawyers are known for having excessive caseloads (particularly in the greater NYC area), sometimes receiving five or more new cases per month (each of which can each go on for years).

These attorneys are working hard but are often overwhelmed, meaning they may forget court dates or have trouble with consistent communication. It would benefit you to ask the attorney if they are on the 18B panel during your consultation so you can assess the full scope of their caseload[32].

It is important to keep an eye out for telltale signs of overwhelm, unresponsiveness, and other red flags that could pop up before or during your consultation. Both objective and subjective factors can play into determining whether or not an attorney is right for you to work with, so use your intuition and ask the right questions.

Is It Important To Work With An Attorney Who Is Familiar With Local Courts?

Choosing to work with an attorney who is licensed in New York is essential, but it is also important to hire an attorney who is familiar with your particular area. In other words, you would want to hire

[32] This is obviously painting with a broad brush. Not all 18B attorneys are insufficient to the task. What I'm speaking to here is a tendency & something to factor into your overall selection process.

a lawyer with an office in Westchester County if that is where your case is based[33].

It is also important to consider that many law firms will bill you for commute time, meaning if one hires a Manhattan attorney to work on a case in Westchester, it will ultimately cost you more money due to hidden commute fees. An attorney should let his/her clients know during an initial consultation whether they will charge for commute time to avoid any surprises.

Additionally, a local lawyer will have better relationships with Judges and be more familiar with local regulations, which can change from county to county in New York. Since there are both written *and unwritten* rules that apply to different jurisdictions, it

---

[33] One attorney I had as a recent adversary admitted – as a Manhattan attorney handling a Westchester case – she felt obligated to hire another Westchester attorney to serve as her co-counsel because she wasn't familiar with the local Judges. This caused drastically increased billing to that client – billing which often exceeded $20,000 per month despite a salary of only about $500,000.

would benefit you to work with an attorney who is familiar with the area where your case is based. This can ultimately save you time and money while putting you in a better position for success.

How Do I Balance Quality And Cost When It Comes To Hiring A Divorce Attorney?

Better attorneys will naturally charge more for their services. It would be wise to have an honest discussion with your attorney about your budget as well as your financial situation. This not only opens the door to discussing payment options, but it can also help to avoid frustration on both ends of the equation in the event you cannot make your retainer payments.

You can discuss different ways to keep costs down and create payment plans, but it is important to have this discussion upfront. For example, discovery is a major point of concern for those looking to cut costs, as many clients accidentally submit discovery that is incomplete and requires multiple follow-ups, each billed to you as the client.

In certain cases, you may want all of the communication with opposing parties to be handled by your attorney. This can quickly become expensive, and I often advise against this if you have financial constraints. In these cases, it is best to attempt having any discussions with opposing parties directly prior to relying on your lawyer for communication.

What Are The Disadvantages Of Choosing An Attorney Solely Based On Their Fees Cost Structure?

If you choose an attorney simply based on their higher hourly rate, you are not guaranteeing they are qualified to handle your case. It is possible you could work with a lawyer who has a nice office in Midtown Manhattan and charges exorbitant fees but gets most of their clients from Google ads and is not fit for your needs. Just because an attorney comes with a high price tag does not mean they are a good choice to handle your case.

However, it is important to take pricing into account as much as any other factors. Some lawyers will charge several hundred dollars more per hour simply because they have a few more years of experience. While experience is an important consideration, it doesn't warrant such a staunch increase in price. It would not be advisable to hire a divorce attorney solely based on their pricing structure without considering other factors such as experience, objective qualifications and proactive communication.

Does Empathy Play A Significant Role In Choosing The Right Divorce Attorney?

I view it as a red flag if an attorney is more worried about the financial aspects of your divorce than they are about the emotional toll it has on your life. For instance, if you are attempting to explain the emotional trauma of discovering your partner sleeping with someone else and your attorney is only focused on your income and assets, that should be a sign something isn't right.

An attorney who shows empathy will try to listen and support you emotionally while helping you navigate the legal minefield of your divorce. Even by encouraging therapy and providing resources for recovery, your attorney can play a pivotal role in helping you rebuild the confidence that you need to navigate your case.

Working with a lawyer who is empathetic toward your situation will not only help you to feel supported and understood but is also a wonderful sign your lawyer will fight to protect your best interests while you are at your most vulnerable.

CHAPTER 28

THE BEST WAYS TO PREPARE FOR YOUR INITIAL CONSULTATION WITH A DIVORCE ATTORNEY IN NEW YORK

Why Is It Important To Consult With A Divorce Attorney?

An initial consultation with an attorney is crucial for determining whether or not you will work well together. By meeting with an attorney, you can see how sympathetic they are to your situation and decide whether or not you'd like to invest in retaining the lawyer. This is a large and expensive commitment, so I would recommend meeting with at least two or three attorneys before making your decision.

You should plan to have several consultations; I would encourage you to shop around the same way you may shop for a new car. Instead of going to a dealership and buying the first car you look at, you would want to do your research and test several vehicles before making a decision.

During your search, you may find certain dealerships that turn you off from wanting to do business or others that stand out for their character. The same principles apply to hiring your divorce attorney, as this is a serious decision with significant financial implications.

What Documents Should I Bring To Meet With My Divorce Attorney?

It is not generally necessary to bring documentation to your initial consultation. You can provide any documents you would like to have reviewed by emailing them to your attorney prior to your consultation. This way, your documents can be reviewed by your attorney prior to your meeting so you will still have time for any questions you may have.

In lieu of your bringing documentation or financial information to our first meeting, I have a standard intake form where I will ask potential clients for basic information such as income, homeowner status, property portfolios and lists of assets.

Am I Allowed To Bring Someone To My Initial Consultation For Support?

You can bring someone to your consultation, but this is not always wise. The primary rule is to never bring your spouse to a divorce consult unless you have cleared this with your attorney. This can easily lead to a conflict of interest for your lawyer and should be avoided unless you and your potential attorney have decided otherwise.

I would also highly recommend clearing any friends or relatives you plan to bring in through your attorney prior to your initial consultation. For example, if you tell me that you would like to bring your brother to your initial consultation, I will ask if they are going to be a witness in the case.

If the answer is yes, I will ask you to consider bringing someone else in, as another attorney may argue that attorney-client privilege has been waived by bringing a witness to the consultation.

Ultimately, it is okay to bring someone to your consultation for emotional support, but it is important to look out for the risk of accidentally waiving attorney-client privilege. If you plan to bring a friend or family member to your consultation, it is best to contact your attorney first so that they can assess the situation.

What Do I Need To Know About New York Divorce Law Before My Consultation?

Much like any other legal case, I believe knowledge is power. The more educated and prepared you can be to handle your case, the better. In fact, I actually have downloadable eBooks on the homepage of my website (www.blivenlaw.net) which you can review for free to educate yourself on your case. The books discuss how to handle divorce and family law cases in New York, and I encourage all of my potential clients to read these books prior to our meeting.

I love it when a potential client visits my office and lets me know they read the books on my website. This takes a lot of the guesswork off of your plate as the client and reassures me as the attorney you are serious about your case and educated on the divorce process. Gathering the proper resources to educate yourself before your initial consultation benefits both you and your attorney.

What Is The Most Effective Way To Communicate My Goals And Concerns To My Attorney?

In my professional opinion, there is a communicational hierarchy - appointments are better than emails, and emails are better than nothing. Emails are useful in certain scenarios, but any lengthy discussions should be reserved for appointments. Luckily, the advent of Zoom and FaceTime makes it easy to schedule appointments and address any questions or concerns.

Appointments are also preferable for financial reasons. I have had back-and-forths with clients who have not realized they are billed separately for each email and text message when they could just as easily address their concerns in a 30-minute meeting. When you have something to discuss at length, an appointment is your best option.

What Are Some Common Mistakes I Can Avoid In My Initial Consultation?

Step one is to avoid telling your potential attorney you have an especially complicated case but can't afford to pay. Very few lawyers agree to take cases pro bono - and they'll likely steer you in the direction of Legal Aid or court-assigned counsel.

Second, you will want to be as honest as possible with your attorney so they can make an assessment of your case based on an accurate account of events. If you don't provide your attorney with accurate, honest information, they may accidentally misrepresent your case.

It is also important to be sure you make a list of any necessary questions you want to get out of the way. This way, you can avoid leaving your consultation feeling like you need to book another one because you forgot to ask important questions.

About The Author

David Bliven graduated with honors from Syracuse University in 1993 with a B.A. in Sociology. He went on to serve as a statistician with the NYS Commission on City Court Judicial Reallocation with the Office of the Deputy Chief Administrative Judge. He then attended New York Law School where he graduated in 1997 with honors and ranked within the top 15% of his class.

Shortly after graduating, he served as a prosecutor for nearly 3 years with the NYC

Administration for Children's Services. While at ACS he prosecuted child support, child abuse & neglect and foster care cases on behalf of the City of New York.

After leaving the prosecutor position, Mr. Bliven opened his present practice in 2000. His practice is currently devoted 100% to Divorce & Family Court cases.

Mr. Bliven has an "AV" rating from Martindale-Hubbell (the highest possible rating in both Legal Ability & Ethical Standards), a perfect 10.0 rating from Avvo ("Superb" rating) and is listed in the "Super Lawyers" directory by Thompson Reuters (a distinction given to less than 5% of all attorneys in each field of practice). He is also a "Certified Financial Litigator" and was honored as a "Super Lawyer" for the NY Metro & Westchester area by *Westchester Magazine* in their October, 2019 issue.

Mr. Bliven has authored the books "Navigating Your New York Divorce Case, "Navigating Your New York Family Court Case" and "Navigating Your New York High Net Worth Divorce Case." His articles have been published in the New York Law Journal, Nolo.com and Westchester Lawyer Magazine.

TESTIMONIALS

- Anonymous: "During a time, when it seemed as my life was about to fall apart, Mr. Bliven was there to make sure I was protected. Mr. Bliven was there to make sure every "T" was crossed and every "I" was dotted. He made sure I was entitled to my fair share. When children are involved in a divorce, I wanted to make sure they were taken care of for the foreseeable future. Mr. Bliven made it his duty to fight for me when he felt I deserved more retribution. He fought tooth and nail for the needs of my children as well as for me. During a time when things looked bleak, Mr. Bliven made sure my legal and financial needs are taken care of. When beginning this venture, I was scared that I would walk off of this with only my "shirt", but Mr. Bliven made it his job to make sure I was able to resume my life without looking back. I want to thank Mr. Bliven and I would recommend him to anyone who is and is thinking about filing for a divorce."

- Jonathan: "Mr. Bliven came very highly recommended to me by a friend who used to practice family law and had transitioned into other areas of legal practice. I was not disappointed. Mr. Bliven was thoroughly knowledgeable and highly attentive as he helped me smoothly resolve complex child support matters involving international issues of competing jurisdictions. Having had a number of attorneys in the course of my divorce and child custody/support matters over the last 18 years, I believe I am experienced to know that Mr. Bliven is a top family law expert."
- Lou: "Mr. Bliven represented me in a child support case. I was very pleased with the services provided by Mr. Bliven. He is professional, courteous, and knows his stuff! I am completely gratified with the outcome of my case. Thanks to Mr. Bliven's knowledge of family law. Mr. Bliven kept me up to date on all

matters pertaining to my case and his billing is fair and accurate for the work he puts into the case. I would certainly recommend him to anyone that is seeking a topnotch lawyer in the area family court."

- Teri Colon: "Although I have not met with Mr. Bliven yet. I contacted his office on a Friday of a Holiday Weekend. His office's response was immediate and I was treated with respect as if I was already a client. His staff took the time to email me immediately and when I called I was given an appointment that accommodates my schedule. Custody matters are very sensitive and clients can be emotional. It was a relief to speak with someone who was not only professional and courtesy, but also showed genuine concern. I look forward to my consultation with Mr. Bliven."
- Ariane: "Mr. Bliven was knowledgeable, informative, and an incredible strategist. He used all of my legal rights to defend me in my case and was extremely professional to work

with. I can't thank him enough for his ability to use our rights as law-abiding citizens and to get the job done. David consulted with me on all motions before revealing them to the court or to any other parties. For this I thank him and am grateful for his diligence in representation."

- Gregg: "Although I subscribe to a legal plan through my union (I'm a teacher), I decided to retain Mr. Bliven based on our initial consultation. He seemed much better versed than the less expensive "plan" attorney I spoke to in the child support matter I brought to him. Mr. Bliven scanned the paperwork I brought with me to the consultation and immediately developed a strategy using various points of law. Mr. Bliven kept in constant contact with me and "cc'd" me on all correspondence he and my ex-wife's attorney had via email or hard-copy. Mr. Bliven's courtroom demeanor was just as I had hoped it would be; vocal and on point. Ultimately, my ex-wife and I reached a fair compromise that did not follow the default percentages NY State dictates. I would definitely retain again should the need arise."

- A Satisfied Client: "Navigating family court for personal reasons can be quite intimidating, even for folks who have interfaced with court officers and judges for professional purposes. That said, Bliven was nothing short of extremely knowledgeable, courteous and very attuned with the emotional experience that comes with the process. I highly recommend Bliven if you are seeking consultation and representation with a child support and/or custody case!"

****

More Testimonials may be found on David Bliven's website (http://www.blivenlaw.net/Testimonials.shtml) and at Avvo (https://www.avvo.com/attorneys/10463-ny-david-bliven-952796.html#client_reviews).

*　　*　　*　　*

If you appreciated the information given to you in this book, Mr. Bliven would appreciate a review of the book on Amazon and/or a Google review:

https://g.page/law-offices-of-david-bliven-933/review?rc

INDEX

S

T

U

V

W

Notes

Made in the USA
Monee, IL
03 November 2026

67387939R10122